Praise

'I found *Destination Animation* engaging and pacy, and liked the balance of information and case studies/examples. The structure will help people to navigate and dip in and out, depending on their process or stage of commissioning. It really does give a fantastic overview. Universities/students/colleges would be a good audience for this great introduction to the stages of a production process.'

— **Kate O'Connor**, Animation UK Council

'I read this as someone who has always wanted to deploy animation, but lacked the tools for advocacy. I now feel equipped to articulate the benefits and the process for attaining them. The abiding impression of *Destination Animation* is that the reader is put in the privileged position of eavesdropping on an otherwise arcane process, with a friendly narrator who is keen to pass on their deep practical knowledge and passion for the subject. The writing is very clear, and the concepts are articulated so that a novice will be able to grasp everything. Overall, it is easy to read, fluid and engaging.'

— **Vanessa Vasani**, Retail Reply

'I enjoyed *Destination Animation*. It definitely gave me a much greater understanding of animation for marketing and communication. The reference to people remembering jingles really resonated for me.'

— **John McMahon**, MCM

Christine MacKay

destination animation

How smart marketeers convey
complex messages memorably

Re think

Cover Design by Emma Rhodes. Sal design by Fred Watts.

To Sandra

'Imagination is more important than knowledge. For knowledge is limited to all we now know and understand, while imagination embraces the entire world.'

– Albert Einstein

Contents

Foreword

The UK's animation sector is known for its quality, humour and inventiveness, as well as leading-edge techniques, creating new worlds and brilliant storytelling. Animators introduce characters that will be the global brands of tomorrow. I'm sure we can all recall animated characters and 'cartoons' from our childhood, and the shows that children love and watch repeatedly today.

Animation is a huge business. It attracts a global audience and is a means of communication. It is used powerfully in advertising, education and business. The animated John Lewis Christmas advertisement is now an anticipated annual event; the COVID-19 pandemic saw animated educational content used increasingly to support online learning.

Destination Animation tells the story of this medium for business-to-business communication. It explores why animation is so compelling, versatile and innovative, illustrating why it is a sharp business tool and how it transcends language and cultural barriers, travels well and converts complex messages and concepts visually. This is incredibly important in our international business marketplace.

Christine has deep first-hand experience, drawing on her hugely creative and varied background of founding and

1

running salamandra.uk, one of the leading business animation studios in the UK with an international client base. One of the book's strengths is that it lays out information to the uninitiated in an unpatronising way, running through the options and applications, the process and production techniques, and the new opportunities through immersive content. Hints and tips and considerations are brought to life by case studies and Christine's direct experience, making it one of those rare books that imparts considerable knowledge in an accessible style.

Aimed at professional marketeers and corporate communications experts, *Destination Animation* will appeal to all who have a message to get across. Film and animation students and teachers will also find this a helpful text. It gives a clear overview and draws on a fantastic range of examples and personal anecdotes to provide a history and production guide as well as a personal account.

As someone who advocates on behalf of this incredible industry, I can say that this book will now become a reference point. I learned from it, will quote from it and highly recommend it.

> **– Kate O'Connor**, Executive Chair,
> Animation UK Council, www.animationuk.org

Introduction

For business, nothing communicates as succinctly and memorably as animation.

I've worked with multinationals, nationals, small and medium sized enterprises, startups and their advertising and public relations agencies, client and agency side, in over eighteen industries and three continents. What I have repeatedly seen is how smart marketeers and business owners improve and often completely revitalise their communication of complex messages through animation. It's an extremely versatile marketing tool which can be used on a variety of platforms.

Marketing decision experts in online, digital and events recognise that in this increasingly always-on environment, animation is a vital tool in their arsenal for internal and external communications, sales and human resources (HR). Its adoption reflects innovation, insight and being open to new ideas.

To illustrate just how powerful a sixty-second animation can be for business, research company Forrester analysed how many words it would take to describe what you might see, feel, hear and understand if you were to view this animation.[1] These words would need to convey all that you experience, including the colours, backgrounds and environments, the narrative or story itself, the denoue-ment, the music, the timbre of voices, the accent, the contents, the emotion conveyed, what you felt and what was memorable.

How many words do you think you would need? A few hundred? A few thousand? Try 1.8 million. Forrester's researcher calculated this number on the premise that a picture paints a thousand words, multiplying thirty frames of video a second by sixty seconds. That's how much information a sixty-second animation can pack in to get your complex messages across succinctly and memorably. Best yet, images stay in the long-term memory, as opposed to text that stays in the short-term memory.

Seeing a gap in the market for a tool that gets business messages across in a snap, I founded salamandra.uk in 2014 to specialise in animation for the business-to-business (B2B) market. Marketing professionals and business owners are always on the lookout for new solutions and ideas to convey complex messages simply and memorably in an environment that is constantly evolving. They need to overcome challenges from over-saturated marketing platforms and the dwindling attention span of target audiences. There are always new things to learn and deal with, while working with the age-old challenges of budget or deadline. Fresh new methods and tools that can be repurposed for a multitude of uses and placed on a variety of platforms will give businesses the best marketing return on investment (ROI).

Businesses need to convey a B2B message in a way that will resonate memorably with target audience(s) and answer their pain points. It needs to positively impact sales targets, bonuses, promotion and budget renewal or increase. By ticking all the right boxes with successful campaigns for online, print, TV, events, presentations and conferences, businesses can create their own marketing halo effect to elevate their status and success.

Marketing professionals and business owners will need to identify a trusted animation supplier or partner to fulfil their marketing needs expertly, outline and agree the cost and timeline, explain how it works and make the right recommendations at all the right milestones. *Destination Animation* is designed to help you with this task.

As a marketing or communications expert, you will likely have several goals for your projects, all of which need to sell your business products or services, differentiate you from the competition and make you the authority in your industry. I hope you will learn to love the medium of animation as much as I do. Animation is like ice cream – mention either and people's eyes tend to light up or it makes them smile. It reminds them of their childhood days. Animation brings joy and fun to those who create it, commission it and watch it. *Destination Animation* will show you how to make it the best and most versatile marketing, sales and communication vehicle in your collection.

Despite its uptake in many industries, animation is still considered something new to help a business stand out from the competition, a nice to have rather than a must have. Essentially, though, 'cartoons' can be serious.

Many businesses are used to using live film footage as a way of representing themselves. Animation is more of an equaliser for the end viewer because it mitigates humans' ingrained instinct to make split-second judgements based on people's faces, as well as the potential woodenness that businesspeople often display on film. Animated caricatures keep businesses' films fun, present their personality and make the overall message engaging.

Animation is visual content that resonates with your target audience(s). *Destination Animation* will expand on how this works and how to create animated visuals, showing you ways of repurposing and 'sweating' an animated asset once it's created. The tried-and-tested 3Ps process of **plan**, **produce** and **publish** will guide you step by step to understand and implement your successful and multiuse end asset – and how it can be used and placed in a myriad of ways. This book will show you how to distil your message verbally, visually and auditorily, picking out what resonates with your target market, as well as how to convey your solution to your audience's pain points via your product or services. It will share the different approaches and platforms for marketing and branding visual solutions, static or animated, and how animation is today's new business jingle.

Nothing communicates your business's message as succinctly and memorably as a well-made animation. *Destination Animation* will show you how to get it created the right way.

PART ONE

THE NEW (VISUAL) JINGLE

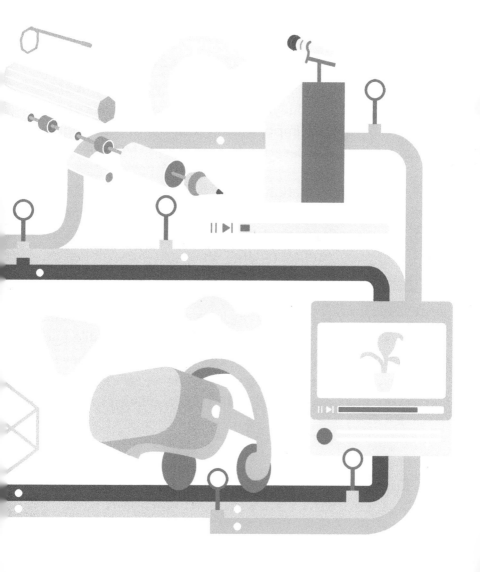

A bit of a marketing relic, a jingle is a short song or tune created for radio or TV advertising. Jingles are a form of sound branding and contain one or more hooks that explicitly promote the product or service being advertised, usually through the use of slogans. These marketing tools have now largely been superseded by pop songs in advertising, but it's hard to forget the 'baba ba baba' from McDonald's 'I'm lovin' it'.

Regardless of being somewhat dated, jingles remain powerful marketing assets. I'm sure you remember a few jingles from your youth, can still sing them, know the words and, more importantly, recall the brand. Jingles may take us back decades, but still feel fresh in our minds.

The power of animation is that it is the modern-day visual equivalent of the jingle. It helps us remember the benefits of a business's product or service, conveying in a snap what it does. And animation visuals stay in our long-term memory.

As soon as you decide to include an animated explainer into your marketing mix, you will see how versatile and powerful this asset can be. And done well, it will have a massive positive effect on your target audiences, as well as your marketing spend, ROI and brand awareness.

chapter 1 ○

Why Animation Is
A Phenomenal B2B Tool

As marketing tools go, there are few more versatile than an animation to help convey complex business and brand messages on any platform.

This tool can be localised and translated for any territory or language. It can be used for websites, presentations, conferences, Zoom calls, email signatures, HR training or inductions, health and safety, sales, social media posts, as part of digital promotions, advertising or public relations (PR). And marketeers can really 'sweat' this asset, repurposing it for various uses.

All marketing budgets are finite. With ongoing pressure for ROI, what better way to spend that budget than on something with so many uses to get your message across successfully, succinctly and memorably?

Often, businesses consider using animation, but don't know where to start or understand what it involves, or indeed what benefits it brings. Once I've taken you through all the various permutations of animation for B2B, you'll see there are few other marketing or communication assets that tick quite as many boxes to engage with your target audiences and get them to take up your call to action (CTA).

Take the well-known online service Dropbox, now a huge company.[2] Dropbox had a rudimentary explainer video made when it was a startup in 2009. Ahead of its time, the company placed this on its landing page for a number of years – it apparently got 30,000 views a day and more than 25 million views in total. This animation was monumental to Dropbox's early growth.

Your guide to B2B animation

Studies have shown that viewers retain 95% of an animated video's message compared to just 10% when they're reading text.[3] Animation is extremely shareable on all business communications and social media platforms. Including one on your landing page can boost your conversion rate by 80% and increase organic search traffic on your website by 157%.

Yet many businesspeople still view animation as light-hearted, reminiscent of Saturday morning cartoons. They don't believe it needs to be taken seriously to help them convey their complex B2B messages to their target audiences.

I don't want you to make the same mistake.

Just as the medium is fabulous for entertainment and story-telling in the Pixar and Disney fashion, it is also incredibly impactful for business messaging and building marketing or brand narratives. Since our cave-dwelling days, humans have been programmed to learn, remember and recount through storytelling. Animation is the modern electronic version.

Here are some of the ways you can use an animation in business. Because there are so many applications and approaches to animation in marketing or communications, I'll mainly be using a standard sixty-second corporate explainer as a benchmark.

An explainer animation is a short, usually one-to-two-minute, video that explains a product, service or brand in an accessible and engaging way. Besides giving proven benefits to search engine optimisation (SEO) and con-versions, an explainer video on your landing page is like being able to give an elevator pitch to every person who passes through your website. You can rely on the video portraying the best impression of your business every time and leaving a memorable message in the mind of the visitor.

As a medium of communication, B2B animation can be used in many ways, including as a corporate explainer video for your executives or sales team, brand content in marketing, presentations and at events, internal or external training, education and communications, HR or health and safety inductions, to name a few. You can place or post your animation front and centre on your website's landing page, or as part of a series of animations explaining different products or services on other parts of your website.

As an induction tool for new and existing staff members, animation enables HR to deliver your elevator pitch in a snap. And remember, your internal team is your best brand ambassador when it comes to evangelising what you do and how you do it. If your people grasp all the facets of the business from your animation, they can articulate this clearly to others while at work or play.

Animation is a marvellous tool to explain all your products or services to new, existing and past clients, potentially introducing them to the whole gamut your business offers, not just what they already know. Current and new suppliers can fully understand what you do and how you do it via animation. You never know, they may turn into clients, too, or refer your services by sharing your animation. As part of a sales presentation, animation ensures uniformity of brand message across divisions, territories and geographies.

Include animations in email campaigns and on all your social media platforms to promote your company and brand. Snippets or looping video sections of the animation are especially useful to highlight particular aspects of your business or service. Why not use snippets for a digital white paper, magazine or blog? And, of course, animation can form part of your credentials deck to send out to prospects.

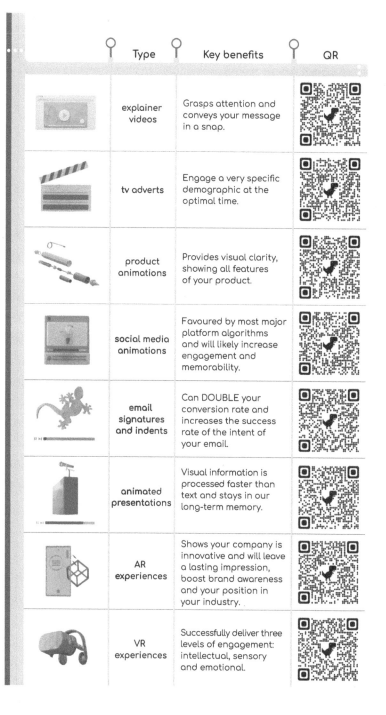

	Type	Key benefits	QR
	explainer videos	Grasps attention and conveys your message in a snap.	
	tv adverts	Engage a very specific demographic at the optimal time.	
	product animations	Provides visual clarity, showing all features of your product.	
	social media animations	Favoured by most major platform algorithms and will likely increase engagement and memorability.	
	email signatures and indents	Can DOUBLE your conversion rate and increases the success rate of the intent of your email.	
	animated presentations	Visual information is processed faster than text and stays in our long-term memory.	
	AR experiences	Shows your company is innovative and will leave a lasting impression, boost brand awareness and your position in your industry.	
	VR experiences	Successfully deliver three levels of engagement: intellectual, sensory and emotional.	

The possibilities appear endless, which shows the power a standard sixty-second corporate animation can have as a communication asset.

What to expect when commissioning an animation

The most important thing to do when you're commissioning an animation is to pick a studio that has a proper briefing process, does its research on your business, your industry and your competitors, and engages you for approvals along the way. A good animation studio will talk you through all these elements and advise you how to repurpose your asset to ensure you get the biggest bang for your buck. Look for one that offers a joined-up service and takes the time to understand your company or product first and foremost. Make sure it has the in-house skills to complete the project and get you to your animation destination.

Animation is a multifaced and highly skilled discipline and a worthwhile investment, so your chosen studio should align with your requirements. If you need any amends in future, or to create a bigger project series, a studio will often be a better option than a freelancer, because a studio will have the capacity to make ongoing changes as well as the archiving potential to keep all your files available.

In my experience, and depending on the complexity, a sixty-second 2D animation will take on average four to five weeks to produce, including the corporate approval processes required from client-side. (More on 2D animation in Chapter 2.) Approval milestones are vital to ensure you (the client) are delighted at every stage and the project is totally aligned to your requirements.

Unlike video, which is about filming what already exists, absolutely everything in animation needs to be created from scratch, with care, flair and precision, from the backgrounds, characters, motions graphics and written call outs, to the music, colours and voiceovers, including engaging the talent (eg voiceover actors) and recording studio time needed to achieve all this. Added to that are the sound effects and the editing and compositing to finish up your polished piece and make it flow to the narrative.

With animation, you have the versatility of taking the narrative into the past or future without mammoth filming, casting and travel budgets. You can go inside a piece of engineering and create a product explosion where the machinery animates apart, allowing viewers to see the various inner parts that make it work in a slick and engaging manner. Animation allows for call-out motion graphics to highlight certain workings or benefits. (There's more on motion graphics in Chapter 2.) It could even go right into an atom or a virus to show how your product, solution or service works, because with animation, anything is possible.

Summary

I consider today's B2B animations to be this era's version of a jingle. An animation is powerful, memorable and, just like a catchy tune, it stays in your long-term memory.

Animation is a versatile medium for bringing complex business and marketing messages, methodologies, solutions, services and products to life in an engaging and memorable way. It can be humorous, serious and everything in between. Animation can really support the marketeer or business owner to get their message across on any platform. It is portable and can be repurposed in a number of ways, giving you an asset that you can 'sweat' to create great ROI.

An explainer animation is a short video that explains a product, service or brand in an accessible and engaging way. Having an explainer video on your landing page is like being able to give an elevator pitch to every person who passes through your website.

When you're commissioning an animation, pick a studio that has a proper briefing process, does its research and engages you for approvals along the way. A good animation studio will advise you how to repurpose your asset to ensure you get the biggest ROI. Look for one that takes the time to understand your company or product and has the in-house skills to complete the project.

This dynamic industry is continually improving and offering new and exciting ways of getting your message across, making animation your most phenomenal B2B marketing tool.

chapter 2

Styles Of Animation

Animation is varied in its uses in business. Its visual approach is equally multifaced, depending on what will resonate and engage with your target audiences best. This is why your animation studio needs to do some desktop research on your business brand specifics, your industry and your competitors so it can present you with an initial variety of suitable visual approaches to be signed off by you and your team.

Using an animated character instead of live film footage of an actual person in a video allows your piece to come across as genderless, cultureless and more sensitive, so you can cover taboo subjects in a way that is difficult using real people. As humans, we are hardwired to make snap decisions about people we come across. It's a natural part of the fight or flight instinct we have among our survival skills. We make instantaneous judgements based on the appearance of people we meet face to face, or see on TV or in magazines and newspapers. In a few nanoseconds, we have already decided a whole 'backstory' for them, their likes and dislikes, whether they are anything 'like us', and hence whether to like, trust, look up to, look down on, listen or not to them.

This does not happen with animation. As it is not 'real', our instincts are not on the same alert, and so we accept the information with fewer preconceived ideas. This means animation can reach, resonate and engage with our target audiences in a less biased way and deliver our messages in an unfiltered and neutral manner.

But what exactly is animation? There are seven main styles of animation: traditional, 2D, 3D, motion graphics (part of 2D), stop motion, augmented reality (AR) and virtual reality (VR). Let's have a good look at each one in turn.

Traditional animation

This is the hand-drawn style. Although an expensive option, traditional animation is still sometimes used in entertainment or shorts (brief films), but is rarely used for corporate animation due to its cost and inflexibility.

In this style of animation, everything is drawn frame by frame. Although beautiful, it is time consuming and does not allow for changes. If you want something edited or tweaked, the whole section needs to be drawn again. This makes it a project that is not easy, quick or cost effective to update.

Walt Disney was famous for perfecting this style in his iconic movies. His most famous hand-drawn epic is *Snow White*, which took around three years to produce with over 750 artists completing more than 2 million sketches.[4]

CASE STUDY – THEIR, THEY'RE, THERE

My team did a pro-bono hand-drawn project for our friends at Resource Productions to help with a young film maker's project. They needed a section to be animated and we decided to use this technique because it best represented a young person doodling on their exam paper, which was part of the narrative. It was a rewarding project and was nominated for several international awards. The filming was done in one day, acted and directed by teenagers. The editing took another day, but the animation took over two weeks.

For this project, salamandra.uk partnered with Director Oliver Blower and Arts Council England to produce a short live action/animation combo. The short was created for Channel 4's *Random Acts* series.

The short, titled 'Their, They're, There', is a media mashup between animation and live action. It conveys Oliver's playful yet painfully honest poem about the familiar frustrations of exams, feeding into themes such as children's mental health, learning disorders and the stigma that surround both. This was particularly poignant during the Covid-19 pandemic, which involuntarily shone a light on alternative teaching styles.

The short shows a boy, Joe, sitting an exam he desperately doesn't want to be taking part in. His stream of consciousness runs wild as his frustration grows at being forced into taking the exam. His antithesis, Jess, is sitting opposite him as she whips through the paper. Joe eventually gives up on the paper, turning to draw his animated thoughts.

The animation process involved having to think about the drawing abilities and age group of the hero. We had to overcome the initial challenge of having the drawings looking too simple, otherwise the art style would be perceived as too young. We also had to think about the media used as well, which affected the line-art and transitions. A student sitting in an exam room wouldn't have access to paintbrushes, so the tools available had to be marker pens, highlighters, biros and coloured pencils. The animation had to reflect this doodled look.

The short was nominated for three awards, and because of the strong messages around challenges in learning and the classroom, it was added to Channel 4's platform #AmINormal, a project that redefines what we think of as 'normal'. Take a look at the short on www.salamandra. uk/news/their-theyre-there-animation-motion-graphics

CASE STUDY – BRAVE NEW GIRL

Another example of how a hand-drawn approach can be the right choice to support the narrative style is Brave New Girl. After creating a successful animated preview for her newest book Brave New Girl,[5] salamandra.uk was commissioned by Lou Hamilton to devise an animation to convey her personal brand and career journey. This project culminated in a forty-five-second piece to add to the book preview and launch her brand, using her existing book illustrations as a blueprint.

In the animation, Brave New Girl, representing Lou's brand and alter ego on various platforms, finds freedom when her children fly the nest. Then, feeling lonely, she sends out messages to cheer herself up. Suddenly she finds herself surrounded by like-minded souls who lift her up, and together as a tribe they fly off to an exciting future. This reflects how Lou's online Brave New You and the Tribe membership club, which is now Brave New Girl podcast, came into existence, furthering her book's publishing success.

Taking the illustrations as our starting point, we set to work on bringing the idea to life visually by choosing a whimsical style that would complement Lou's delicate drawings with their powerful punch. We picked a hand-drawn style to support the original way the illustrations have been created in her books and on social media. This frame-by-frame process is long and labour intensive, but it rendered the right emotional intensity and storytelling needed for this subject.

Careful sound design was created by identifying complementary music and animating to its cadence. The subtle use of the right sound effects completed it and helped to tug at the heartstrings for a sweet and engaging piece.

Turning the Brave New Girl brand into a living and breathing animation using a hand-drawn style worked well in conveying the writer's personality and was a finalist in the Moondance International Film Festival. To take a look, please visit www.salamandra.uk/news/brave-new-girl-animation

2D animation

Arguably the most common style of corporate animation is the repurposable 2D vector-based visual asset. This represents graphics that are created in two-dimensional programs such as Adobe Photoshop or Illustrator software. While these graphics can be manipulated to look three dimensional, if you can't rotate the object to get multiple views, you are working with a 2D animation. Possessing only width and height (no thickness), 2D elements are either (infrequently) hand drawn or created on computers.

This kind of animation is quicker to produce. With the advances of video effects and storyboarding software, it's becoming easier than ever to create 2D visual assets that can often be less draining on your studio's machines than 3D software.

The benefits of choosing 2D for your project include:

o   Cost effectiveness. The main cost factors that determine your price tag include the amount of detail in the design, complexity of the animation, film length, voiceover and music. For animation cost parameters, expect to pay anything from a few thousand to tens or sometimes hundreds of thousands, depending on the complexity.

o   2D animations are faster to produce because they are flat images, so less labour intensive.

o They can be easy to update, particularly compared to live-action film where you need to get the whole crew back and recreate the same conditions as the previous shoot. And because 2D is less complex than 3D, updating corporate assets later is more feasible, potentially giving them a longer shelf life.

o 2D animations can be adapted to print and web-based materials because they are already created in a two-dimensional space. They can easily be transformed into static graphic design elements for your website, PowerPoint presentations, infographics and printed corporate collateral such as brochures, business cards etc. Repurposing your asset in this way ensures uniformity of visual messaging and helps build brand awareness through consistent and recognisable visual assets.

2.5D animation

If you like the aesthetic of a 3D animation, but lack the budget or the timeline requirements, there is another option for you to pick. It's a happy medium called 2.5D. In essence, it is a 2D animation that is manipulated to look like a 3D animation. Technically, your studio can create an optical illusion with tools such as layering, shadowing and mass/weight to give 2D animations the same type of movement as 3D.

3D animation

One of the main perceived differences between 2D and 3D is that the former is more artistic and the latter more mechanical. It can be the case that a 2D animation is flowy and illustrative, and a 3D animation is realistic and physically accurate, but just as easily, a 2D animation can be technical and a 3D animation can be stylised, fluid and over accentuated. It purely depends on the subject matter and style of animation.

When we're referring to the actual production of the animation itself, the two are quite similar, but in 3D you are working in an extra dimension. Both types of animation work at the simplest level by inputting the position, scale and rotation of an object at any given point in time (this is in the form of something called a keyframe). There are obviously more levels to it than that, but at the base level, 2D and 3D animation share that central idea.

Where 2D may require more illustration, 3D works with 'rigs' (more on this in Chapter 7) and the models are given a skeleton that can be manipulated, posed and repurposed in unlimited fashion. Basically, 3D gives your audience a three-dimensional view of the environment. But not all 3D models are rigged. Rigs are only applied to elements that need to have individual parts that move, for example characters or complex objects that need more control.

Graphics that are modelled in a three-dimensional environment, and then animated are called 3D animations.

A studio can rotate your assets around in 360-degree space to get whatever angle you want for the composition. This is great when you're showcasing engineering workings of a machine or an architectural 'fly-through', for example.

Modelling 3D scenes, objects and characters to create visuals is called computer-generated imagery (CGI). Often when we view films that are created in CGI, because they look so realistic, we don't even realise they are animated. It's worth pointing out that CGI, although it technically covers all imagery generated with a computer, including 2D, is generally accepted to reference realistic 3D animation that is intended to be indistinguishable from reality. However, some people use it to cover all 3D animation, realistic or otherwise. Also, while 3D predominantly uses realistic lighting and perspective, the style of the assets doesn't have to realistic. Some brilliant results can be achieved in 3D with stylisation rather than realism – just look at Pixar!

The benefits of 3D include:

o   Eye-catching visual appeal that can take your business message to the next level.

o   It's a dynamic format. Because it operates in a three-dimensional space, it offers more options for visual narration, and due to the advances in software and technology, the creative options are becoming limitless.
    You can create animated mock-up versions

of a new or upcoming product from every angle, highlighting every feature with a photorealistic render for your audiences' ultimate digital viewing experience. Being able to showcase assets that don't yet exist or are hard to portray in real life can engage your potential customers and drive conversions for beta products ahead of completion.

o If you are thinking of creating a series, then 3D animations might give a better ROI than 2D. Though more expensive to produce initially, 3D can easily be repurposed into a variety of assets. You can show the same elements from different 'camera' angles and take as many still renders as you need from whatever angle and lighting set up you require, or swap out a material and easily re-render. A good example is the IKEA catalogue, where most 'photos' are actually 3D renders.

o 3D offers interactive options, and there are exciting platforms that allow for real-time interaction in your animations. Much like 2D animations can be easily repurposed for digital and print collateral, 3D animations can be repurposed for interactive options. Take, for example, home or office remodelling – this is much easier to imagine as a 3D model than a 2D floor plan. The 3D models used in an explainer animation can be designed to be an interactive feature on your website, giving a full view of the remodelling option. Take a look at the interactive 3D map salamandra.uk created for the Royal Albert Hall at www.salamandra.uk/news/royal-albert-hall-interactive-map

Artistically labour intensive, 3D animation has various roles within it, such as modeller, texture artist, lighting artist, rigger, animator and compositor (more on this in Chapter 8), working through a complex pipeline of techniques and special effects such as lighting and texturising. If you're choosing 3D, make sure that your studio has the in-house skills and calibre required.

Motion graphics

Motion graphics are bits of animation creating the illusion of motion or rotation which your studio will combine with audio for your multimedia projects. Using text as a major component, they are essentially animated graphic design blended together with sounds.

This is a great way to communicate with your audience and adds depth to your animation. Motion graphics can be combined with any 2D or 3D project, and together with music and effective copy, they help convey your complex message. They're often used to create adverts, or in title sequences for corporate explainers (or TV programmes and movies) to share information.

Your animation will need to be content rich to include as much information as it can fit into a sixty-second piece without overwhelming your viewers. Motion graphics added in will support the narrative with text 'call outs' to highlight sections of a business process or explain segments of a piece of engineering.

This style of animation is good for explaining complex ideas because it clarifies abstract, intangible and difficult concepts. Motion graphics can also mitigate the risk of your brand looking too cartoony. As it's a simple option to execute, it is possible to get a good result on a limited budget, as opposed to animations using characters with all their time-consuming elements. But make sure motion graphics resonate with your brand personality. If humanising your narrative is important, consider combining several of the approaches described here.

Stop motion

When you're considering how to animate your B2B communication, stop motion is one of your options. This type of animation uses real-life objects that are moved in small increments and photographed. The slight movements are then combined into a video, creating an illusion of continuous motion.

Stop motion has been used in animated movies, music videos and shorts for years, but the creation process is complicated and tends to take a lot of time. Each individual movement of an object must be photographed separately, so it takes hundreds of slight adjustments to create a convincing illusion that the object is moving on its own.

It is a gorgeous technique, but it comes at a price. You need a dedicated space, continuous uniform light, time, patience and effort to make the most of this technique, hence why it is one of the most expensive styles in animation. Photographing every movement of an object also complicates the process of making any changes to the finished film further down the line. These will result in delays and more cost investment, and sometimes the changes are not possible at all.

For stop motion, you can use any object that cannot move on its own, from illustrated images to food, household implements or plasticine 'puppets', such as the iconic Wallace and Gromit. The main benefit is innovation – stop motion creates a unique animation and helps you stand out. It boosts your brand image and conversions – the originality stays in your audience's memory, and has the quality of being thought provoking and inspiring, so it motivates viewers to share your content with friends and family.

Stop motion is great for explaining tedious concepts and information in a fun and memorable way. From clarifying how a product works to introducing a new health and safety priority, you can hasten the time frames as much as you like because stop motion can be incredibly inspirational, conveying something in a new way which cannot be achieved in real life. The only limit is your creativity.

AR animation

AR allows your brand to give your customers unique experiences simply by using their mobile or tablet devices. Now there's no need to download an app to enable it, AR is becoming increasingly used for business. A great example is Yorkshire Tea's totally immersive and interactive AR experience around environmental sustainability, which you can take a look at on https://youtu.be/Lba--qJzzBk

AR benefits include:

o Try before you buy – from fashion to cosmetics and cars, business to customer (B2C) augmented shopping experiences enable your clients to model your products on themselves.

o Travel and tourism can expand brand experience by adding a digital component to physical locations and products with tailored or bespoke information. Concert halls and theatres use this tool to showcase what the view is like at a venue when customers buy tickets (for an example, see StubHub at www.stubhub.co.uk). Or why not 'fly' through a housing development, taking in the community before it's even been built?

o Augment branding materials take your business cards and brochures to the next level by adding virtual components and animations. Users can scan printed materials with their mobile or tablet devices to access a range of features, giving them more information and an immersive way to experience or connect with your brand.

o Enhance the status of your brand by creating unexpected fun experiences to get people talking and sharing your content within your target audiences. You can even have animations jumping out from an industry catalogue!

AR technology adds layers of digital information on to the physical world in various ways, the most common being the **marker-based AR** experience using a static image or QR code. This marker is scanned by your audience's smartphone camera, redirecting them to a browser-based WebAR experience or an AR app. The scan triggers the 3D animated digital layer.

As technology advances, AR becomes more accessible in our everyday lives and interaction with it more frequent. This will only increase as what was once expensive hardware becomes affordable and readily available. One of the biggest barriers for marketeers to use AR is the misconception that it requires customers to download an app, which is no longer the case for a lot of AR applications that can run directly in most mobile phone browsers.

Life is full of whammies. The Covid-19 pandemic has been the biggest one of my lifetime, but it did advance everyday use of AR. The rise of track and trace apps through necessity following the eruption of the pandemic made scanning QR codes a daily occurrence within cafés, bars and other public places, and as a result, people of all ages are well equipped with the knowledge of QR code usage.

More and more digital natives are entering the business world with the expectation of being able to interact with digital collateral (and print collateral, for that matter). According to research, up to 73% of B2B buyers are now millennials.[6] This generation of buyers has repeatedly shown they expect the same kind of intimacy, immediacy and coherency as their favourite B2C brands offer, so marketing using immersive experiences such as AR is vital.

AR has specific advantages for B2B. The most forward-thinking companies are utilising AR in a wide variety of applications, such as training, demos, sales and interactive print collateral.

Training and demos

AR can be powerful when combined with real-world objects and equipment as a training tool, for example, tracking information over what you are seeing and 'X-ray' or product explosion visualisations on to an actual product. Used in training, this could be particularly beneficial for employees working in dangerous or remote environments, such as people who work in offshore energy.

AR allows for training to be overlaid on to equipment without trainers needing to be present. It also allows your trainees to practise skills in a realistic environment, training to be conducted almost anywhere, and is more cost effective than hiring or using the equipment. This can be great for pharma demonstrations, HR and health and safety training in dangerous environments, for example fire-safety training, and educating on topics like sustainability.

Sales

AR can be used in the word of sales as it presents an opportunity for product-specific information or visualisations to be triggered by and tracked to products. Customers can 'see' a product in their own space, a technique used by companies like IKEA and Dulux. IKEA has released an AR furniture app for phone platforms which lets customers see how their own rooms would look furnished with signature IKEA products.

For B2B, AR can show solutions or products in workplaces or retail spaces. AR can also be used with interactivity to allow users to see how variations on a product, such as changing colours and finishes to a car or furniture, would look in their environment.

Interactive print collateral

For service-based companies, an AR business card can be an opportunity to create a memorable experience, be that educational or relating to your industry. For example, fire-safety tips overlaid on to the environment, or architectural overlay with blueprint-style labels, or something that's more fun and brand-culture related such as bringing a mascot to life. AR can also be used on print collateral such as magazines, leaflets, event banners/stands, or tracked to digital collateral, such as an email campaign or signature, for a more sustainable approach.

Whether you use AR for internal communications, training or in your marketing strategy, it provides a more interactive, engaging and memorable experience for your target audience. In an article from *Pharma Voice*, Sanjiv Mody, CEO and founder of Pixacore, says, 'Augmented reality with the right content and with the right use case can be very engaging. It is not a replacement for a traditional presentation, but AR certainly adds dimension and interactivity to current methods.'[7] AR not only positions your company as creative, innovative and full of personality, but it will leave a lasting impression and hopefully a smile on the face of your clients, customers or employees, boosting your brand awareness and position in your industry.

VR animation

There have been some challenges to using the VR platform, from high cost to build and delivery times, and users' discomfort because of motion sickness. However, VR can speed up your sales funnel by having your customers experience and evaluate your product or methodology in a safe environment. You can bring in avatars of your sales and technical people to be 'present' and help to field questions and close the deal virtually – no matter where in the world your customers might be.

Because VR is totally created digitally, you can design any experience you wish to fit in with your brand or marketing message or product content. This is powerful because your client will be fully immersed in the journey you have created for them to experience, with your communications team's total control, allowing them to get a feel for and play with an exact replica of your product. The good news for marketeers is that VR presentations can be measured for analytics in real time to determine what interests a customer most about a product, what parts of the presentation are most engaging and which customers seem ready to buy.

Historically, technical sales, whether pharma, engineering or construction, required site visits and trade shows to demo how the product or service would work. VR can now accomplish this just by the client using a headset. When you consider the cost of the headset (which the hardware companies have been falling over themselves to make more affordable) versus the cost of a plane ticket, conference ticket or accommodation for your clients, VR clearly makes your demos or expos much more accessible and immersive. All this while mitigating the need for your clients to take time away from home.

Immersive realities in business

Introducing immersive technologies in B2B businesses can offer engagement on three levels:

o Intellectual – serving up useful and relevant knowledge about your business or service

o Sensory – building an environment that resonates with your target audience

o Emotional – giving your target audience a sense of connection and presence with your environment and solutions

The impact that immersive technologies can have is powerful, converting an original prospect into a tangible and integral resource. From startups to huge companies like Apple, VR is changing the way industries move. Over 43% of manufacturing companies say VR will become mainstream in their organisations by 2022.[8] This goes for AR too, even more so as it is already widely implemented. These stats highlight the benefits of using AR and VR successfully, with 82% of companies who have implemented these saying they have exceeded expectations with increased efficiency and productivity.

Using VR in business provides a plethora of different opportunities. It can be used for event demos, to show off products, and at its best, at events to create virtual spaces to expand a user's experience. As for going big scale with events, the endless possibilities of VR platforms can create full-on experiences, making the event more immersive for delegates. This guarantees fulfilment for the attendees, even those who can't physically attend. They can attend virtually and buy merchandise online.

Creating a full virtual event can help you reach out to people globally who may be restricted from travelling by their calendars or finances, opening a whole new world of possibilities. In a virtual world, there's no need to budget for speakers, food and other logistics to host people; that all falls straight into the attendees' hands. Adding VR to an existing event or presentation brings a new layer to the show, breaking the boundaries of what you can and can't do, as well as when people can take part because it can all be pre-recorded and experienced at will.

In B2B, when you're looking to add value to your business or brand, AR/VR can be both an appealing and challenging option. Luckily, some of the worries, such as connectivity and latency, are being overcome by innovative technology moving forward so quickly.

Something that helps AR and VR develop so quickly is – another abbreviation – artificial intelligence (AI). AI and machine learning tools are helping virtual worlds become more sophisticated day by day, allowing computers to 'see' through cameras, which is essential for the user's field to be identified and built on using algorithms.

Immersive realities are exciting fields to adopt as part of your marketing, events and PR. They are tapping into the business sector with potential to grow rapidly and change the way we work, buy, sell and promote products, services and businesses. In a few years, we're likely to look back and wonder how we ever lived without them.

Summary

As humans, we are hardwired to make snap decisions about people we come across as a natural part of the fight of flight instinct we have among our survival skills. In a few nanoseconds, we have already decided whether to like, trust, look up to, look down on and listen (or not) to them.

This does not happen with animation. As it is not 'real', we accept the information with fewer preconceived ideas, so animation can reach, resonate and engage with our target audiences in a less biased way.

There are seven main styles of animation:

o Traditional: the hand-drawn style, rarely used for corporate animation due to its cost and inflexibility.

o 2D: arguably the most common style of corporate animation, this represents graphics that are created in two-dimensional programs such as Adobe Photoshop or Illustrator software.

o 3D: similar to 2D, but you are working in an extra dimension.

o Motion graphics are bits of animation creating the illusion of motion or rotation which your studio will combine with audio. Here, sounds, motion and graphic design blend together well. They are a great way to communicate with your audience and add depth to your animation.

o Stop motion uses real-life objects that are moved in small increments and photographed. Although expensive, stop motion animations are unique, which encourages brand ambassadors to share them more widely.

o AR allows your brand to give your customers unique experiences simply by using their electronic devices. Millennials, who make up a large proportion of B2B buyers, have repeatedly shown they expect the same kind of intimacy, immediacy and coherency as their favourite B2C brands offer, so marketing using immersive experiences such as AR is vital.

o VR can speed up your sales funnel by having your customers experience and evaluate your product or methodology in a safe environment. It can help you reach out to people all around the world who may be restricted from travelling by their calendars or finances.

Now you know the styles of animation that are out there, which style of explainer video should you choose for your business?

chapter 3

Which Animation Style?

Thinking about all the approaches to animation is similar to watching your favourite movie and appreciating how the director has used different styles to achieve the end result, from where it was filmed to the genre (eg western or futuristic – or both), the actors, the music and the colour gradient. All these build up the feeling of the movie that you experience: the tension, excitement, pathos and denouement.

Any style of explainer video can be used for any business type; it just depends on your tone and manner as a brand, the personas of your target market, and what will resonate with them. But it can be overwhelming when you're figuring out what would work for you, so here are some hints.

The quick guide to picking your animation style

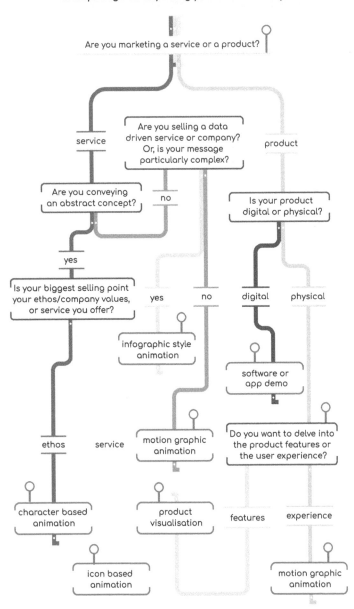

Character-based explainer videos

If you don't have a specific product to sell, or you feel your company's biggest selling point is its ethos or personal service, a character-based explainer video can be a real winner. Friendly and sometimes humorous, these work well for more abstract strategic concepts such as reliability and trustworthiness. A character-based video would be great to illustrate your company's core values, for example.

Character-based animations can also be a great way to highlight how your product or service is essential in your consumer's life, demonstrating relatable scenarios. Characters can be fitted to your target personas, or conversely, designed to avoid any association to a particular geography, culture or ethnicity, making the video relatable to people around the world. Using animals, aliens or even personified objects in situ is a good way to achieve the latter.

A common misconception with character-based explainer videos is that they are always childish or cartoony – this need not be the case at all. Characters can be styled to fit your brand image perfectly, whether it be sober and professional or quirky and irreverent. You could even have avatars of your team or mascot and build on their personality.

Software or app demo

On the other end of the scale is the software or app explainer. You have a concrete product to explain, and it's probably highly technical. You could, of course, record a screencast with your voice behind it, but nothing lets a high-tech solution down more than an amateur presentation.

When physical products are photographed for ads, they are lit, polished and digitally tweaked to perfection to give the best impression. Your software or app deserves the same attention. App or software demos usually involve showing the main features in a stylish three-dimensional animated way. These demos can then be used on landing pages or website feature pages as a video or embedded as a short animation to play automatically.

CASE STUDY – INFOSUM

salamandra.uk client InfoSum developed a world-leading federated data platform enabling advertisers, media owners, providers and other advertising technology firms to collaborate across multiple sources without requiring the underlying data to be moved or pooled while adhering to General Data Protection Regulation. But the company needed help conveying its complex message.

We created a ninety-second explainer animation on InfoSum's data onboarding service, which is where the company shares data between a consumer and a brand without it being transferred over the cloud, thus ensuring security. Realising that this is a complex topic, InfoSum wanted an easy-to-understand video to explain its offering and communicate the benefits of the service while adhering to its brand guidelines and limited colour palette.

The corporate explainer animation we created was technical enough to show InfoSum as a trusted tech professional, but simple enough to convey the complex concept clearly at any level. We started by wrapping our heads around InfoSum's concept before creating a storyboard which conveyed the way we would represent the narrative.

The animation itself shows a continuously moving camera shot from left to right to portray the constant flow of data and the journey of the customer, making it a successful visual method of storytelling. Throughout, we incorporated InfoSum's complex iconography and colour palette of six green tones to stay on brand. It was satisfying taking a text-heavy technical concept and simplifying it with an effective animated visual. You can take a look at the animation by visiting www.salamandra.uk/our-work/infosum

Icon-style explainer video

If you feel a character-based animation is not for you, but you still need to convey more abstract concepts, consider an icon-based animation. This makes use of imagery in icon form to convey the sentiment without assigning it to any persona, which could be a good solution if you are planning on distributing across different languages or cultural backgrounds.

Icons are great for helping viewers instantly associate offerings with visual cues, such as a syringe for medicine or a padlock for security.

Infographic-style explainer video

For a data-driven product, service or company, an info-graphic-style animation can be perfect. This style is a great way to spice up what could be dry information or a complicated message and engage target audiences.

In infographic-style animations, graphic layouts are used to pull out the key information you want the viewer to take away, giving them the visual aid to make sure that information sticks. This style can be helpful when you have strict brand guidelines to adhere to, because much of the visual elements are typographic and can be designed around your marketing framework.

While these techniques touch on motion graphics as an animation style, what we are referring to predominantly here is the use of motion graphics overlaid on film footage. This can be an effective way to add interest to the traditional video formats, such as talking heads or interviews. Graphics can be used as title cards to introduce topics, with interviewee names, with type to highlight key words and phrases being said, or with diagrams or animations to illustrate and emphasise points. Techniques such as motion tracking – tracking the movement of objects and processing the data – can be used to integrate graphics into the scene and keep the format up to date.

This style is well suited to brands that use film, talking heads and photography as their principal house style, but want to take this a step further to better communicate messages. There are many ways motion graphics can be used with film footage. You can take a look at some examples at www.salamandra.uk/our-work/qa

Product visualisation animations

Product visualisations using photorealistic 3D stills or animation are a great way to present cross-sections or exploded views, and can be created before the product is even made. These are impactful for use on any platform or branding collateral, allowing your clients to experience your technical products from every angle and understand their core benefits and minute detail before buying them.

How will you use your animation?

As a next step, think how you will use your style of animation. Will it be for brand awareness, training, induction or advertising? The method used to build your animation will be an important factor in its final usage.

For example, will it be a one-plane flat animation, or will it be using AR so that the piece comes out of the screen

destination checklist

what

- What is your goal or call to action?
- What should your tone of voice be?
- What message do you want your target audience to take away from the animation?
- What are you trying to achieve?
  Eg. is it brand awareness, education, lead generation?

where

- Where will your animation be seen?
- Will the sound play automatically?
- Where will your video hyperlink to?
- What is the optimal size for your platform?
- How much time will the audience have to take it in?

who

- Is your animation for international audiences?
- Where does the animation fit on your customer journey and where will it direct them to?
- Will it need to be translated, subtitled or culturally agnostic?

why

- Does your company have a core message and values that you want conveyed in the animation?
- Why is your company the brand of choice for your customers?

how

- How much will you be investing in the animation and how will you track your return on investment?
- How will you measure the success of your animation?

or the printed collateral in a 3D environment that viewers can 'anchor' into their real surroundings and walk around and interact with? Or will it be used with a VR headset, your audience totally immersed in a 360-degree experience where everything is created in animation?

Consider also the voiceovers required to bring the animation and/or characters to life. What is the perfect voice timbre or accent? Would a male, female or child actor work best? Like film actors, voiceover artists need to be convincing. They must convey your message succinctly in a short space of time, because an ideal word count for a sixty-second animation ranges from 70–100. Can you sum up your business or service in under 100 words?

You need to consider the tone of voice of your animation because it should match your corporate brand guidelines. That said, it is always good to have your animation studio inject personality and perhaps humour into the piece to offer a relatable humanity that your viewers will buy into.

CASE STUDY – ARTEMIS

A good example of finding the right tone of voice is the work salamandra.uk did with Artemis Fund Managers Ltd. This company works with complex financial products and needs to get its messages across to independent financial advisors at their own level. Artemis was uncertain that using animation as a platform would portray its complex financial messages at the right intellectual level.

My team fully grasped the highlighted product before we embarked on the project, because without understanding our clients' products or services, we can't create their visual narrative. This requires asking the right questions during the briefing process to ensure we understand what they do, who their target audiences are and what pain points are being answered by their products.

Despite finance being a serious subject within a corporate company, my team at salamandra.uk injected some tiny elements of humour to make the piece less a B2B message and more a human-to-human (H2H) message. For example, one of the animations talked about retiring and getting old, and showed an elderly man settling down into a wheelchair, but as he sits down, there's a little squeaking spring sound. This subtle touch of humour didn't detract from the seriousness of the subject matter, but made it more engaging and memorable.

You can take a look at more examples by visiting www.salamandra.uk/our-work/artemisglobal

There are many approaches to B2B animation. A good animation studio will guide you expertly on what your narrative needs to look, sound and feel like to get your complex messages across.

Summary

With the many approaches and styles that you can use on all the platforms on offer, there is a plethora of solutions to convey your complex B2B messages using animation. These include:

O Character-based videos, which work well if you don't have a specific product to sell or your company's biggest selling point is its ethos or personal service.

O Software or app demos are at the other end of the spectrum, working well if you have something specific to sell, especially if it's highly technical.

O An icon-style explainer video is worth considering if you feel a character-based animation is not for you, but you still need to convey abstract concepts.

O Infographic-style explainer videos can be perfect for a data-driven product, service or company. This style of animation is a great way to spice up potentially dry information or complicated messages and engage target audiences.

O Product visualisation using photorealistic 3D stills or animation is a great way to present cross-sections or exploded views. The animation can even be created before the product is made.

Any style can be used for any business type; it just depends on your tone and manner as a brand, the personas of your target market, and what will resonate with them. Consider how you will use your animation, because the method you choose to build it will be an important factor in its final usage.

Now we've had a good look at the styles and techniques you can apply to your animation, let's delve into its applications and benefits in branding and marketing.

chapter 4

B2B Marketing's Indispensable Tool

In this chapter, we'll take a deeper dive into the applications and benefits of animation in business branding and marketing for specific roles, sectors and industries.

As a marketeer, you have several tools at your disposal, but few are as versatile as animation. It can be used on so many platforms, from a website to a fundraising presentation, and can be created fully remotely. It can be revised and adapted in the future without the need to rebook a full film crew and make sure the conditions are exactly the same as the first shoot. Because it is all created, it can be edited, improved or updated at any time.

Animation is created as a moving asset, but elements can be extracted as static images which can be repurposed for printed collateral or online articles. This keeps your look and feel uniform, echoing throughout your collateral to illustrate your complex set of business messages continuously and memorably.

Why animation has become a vital tool

Animation simplifies your complex messages and ideas for clarity, while animated characters and environments provide an infinite scope for originality and creativity. What's better than fantasy to capture the interest of your audiences and engage with as many people as possible? This is particularly useful for startups in their early stages when they need to showcase what is new or may not even yet exist while asking for funding.

As animations convey emotions effectively because they interact with their audiences at different levels of perception, combining visual and sound elements at the same time, they build connection, offering viewers aesthetic appeal and allowing the brand to interact with its audience on a more personal level. Studies have shown that a viewer retains 95% of a video's message versus just 10% when they're reading text.[9]

Then there are the timeless and flexible qualities to animation. Filming live actors or business owners can be personable, but that content can date quickly due to staff churn or fashions in clothing or interiors. Conversely, animation stays timeless and can be updated along with the evolution of the business in a cost-effective way.

Animated videos help your business rank higher on Google. Including one on your landing page increases conversion by 80%.[10] According to VNI Global IP Traffic and Service Adoption Forecasts[11] for 2017–2022, created by Cisco, by 2022, the video will account for up to 80% of all traffic compared to 67% in 2014.[12] Even better, conversion rate can be boosted by up to 80% by including a video on the landing page, thereby increasing your brand exposure and client stickiness potential.[13]

Animation is easy to distribute because people love to share interesting content with peers, experts in your field, and friends and family. If viewers like the content, they will look further into the company, thereby raising brand awareness and recognisability for further sales lead conversions, helping you reach your target conversion goals.

Animation is also a great way to inject clarity into training, as we can see from this case study.

CASE STUDY – DELIVEROO

During the Covid-19 pandemic and the resultant lockdowns, animation remained a good fit for business on many levels. In this case study, we will focus on Deliveroo and its explainer/training animation.

During lockdown, among the few services that could still function, and even flourish, were delivery companies, as demand for home deliveries grew exponentially. Deliveroo needed to expand its workforce overnight and its directors were battling to keep up with training, as well as keeping their employees abreast of any new developments to the company's service or apps. They urgently needed an animation explaining a new feature on the software. This feature informs Deliveroo riders and drivers of the optimum way of delivering their orders while getting new orders in the same area, thereby saving the company time and money while allowing the riders to increase what they earn.

At salamandra.uk, we were briefed by Deliveroo's UK operations team, who keep deliveries running smoothly and deal with the logistics to ensure everything works well for their riders. Many riders do not speak English as a first language and a lot of Deliveroo's communication is text based, which posed a problem – one which animation can solve.

The operations team asked us to create an engaging training animation which explains Deliveroo's 'zone clusters' in an easy-to-digest fashion – pun intended! After we had created a mood board, we moved on to create a storyboard which consisted of illustrations or images for the purpose of pre-visualising the animation. From there, we put together a spicy sixty-second animation to explain zone clustering using a technique which creates a 3D illusion in 2D. In our animation, our seemingly 3D rider cycles through a map, showing how to use the app for zone clusters, while the voiceover explains what they are doing.

Throughout the animation, we created a turning camera effect which allowed us to deliver smooth transitions in a creative yet subtle manner while not distracting from the message of the animation. Despite the short deadline, it was a fun project which we delivered on time and in budget, thanks to our robust internal systems.

You can take a look by visiting www.salamandra.uk/our-work/deliveroo

Animation explaining sensitive subjects

It can be difficult for marketeers to tackle sensitive subjects such as abuse, both physical and psychological, humanitarian emergencies, traumatising medical conditions, post-traumatic stress disorder, environmental issues etc. The immediacy and resonating power of animation can evoke empathy and pathos to get the viewers to experience an emotional change and take the CTA required.

A powerful Danish piece called 'Mask'[14] to raise awareness of child abuse is extremely effective in eliciting the intended emotion in the audience, even across the language barrier, illustrating how animation can shift a viewer's mood and change their perception. Although I don't speak Danish, I still got the message.

It's important that your clients feel comfortable with the services you provide, which is why some businesses use animation to build trust with their viewers. As an example, Skills for Care used animation for its marketing campaign 'Stop, Think, Dignity'.[15] This covers how some clients are unknowingly being disrespected by staff members. The viewer watches as an experienced care worker introduces an apprentice starting their first day in the field. Slowly, we notice how the experienced care worker makes the apprentice feel uncomfortable, and then suddenly, we're shocked at how disturbingly familiar the scenario looks.

It's an emotional campaign tackling the subject of disrespect. The business has used this excellent marketing tool to make its brand feel more trustworthy by bringing awareness to the topic. The animation is also used to inform Skills for Care staff on how to treat vulnerable people, and on its marketing and social media campaigns.

Animation explaining complex subjects

Animation really does give you the freedom to convey anything, no matter how complex or dry the subject matter. And it can be done in an entertaining and light-hearted way.

The trick is to 'show', not 'tell' when you're conveying something complex. Use colours and imagery that reflect the topic, visual cues and interesting characters. The script can be pared right down to key words, condensing the content to make it memorable. This will keep the animation short and pithy and retain your audience's attention. And bringing in some humour adds a human touch to your messaging. Because your viewer has a reaction (eg smiles or laughs), the message is more likely to engage with them and stick in their minds.

Benefits of animation for marketing and sales

The global trend for working from home has brought many challenges for marketeers in business. One of them is being heard through the increasing noise in your markets. How do you reach your target audiences when everyone else is trying to do the same, and on the same platforms? Here's where animation can become your most important and versatile marketing tool to get your complex messages across succinctly and memorably.

In an era when we are all time poor, but need to absorb an increasing amount of information to stay ahead, video is grabbing the attention of many eyeballs, usually with the sound off if the viewer is watching in a busy home or office, or during a commute on public transport. If their interest is piqued, they may well watch again later with the sound on.

Animation can be created remotely by people who don't have to be working under the same roof, or even in the same country. Unlike film that needs to reflect the real world, animation is a tool that can be used for several purposes by being abstract or using other representation for human characters. You can create a message that is genderless, neutral to colour or creed, and tackles taboo or difficult subjects such as funerals, violence or abuse. And it can represent the past, the present or the future, showing a company's history or timelines. An animation can also be made into a series without having to re-do a film shoot.

In a survey done on 570 unique businesses, 85% found that animation was an important factor in their strategic marketing, with 76% saying that using an explainer video increased their sales performance.[16] Your only limit is your studio's imagination to get your complex messages across in a way that engages your target audience, so I encourage you to find a studio that really gets under the skin of your business and understands your product or services. If your animators recognise who your target audiences are and what their pain points are, they'll know how to answer them in your messaging as well as ensuring they respond to a CTA. This could be as simple as your target audiences recognising your brand or product, or it could be to encourage them to find out more and connect with your team.

Whether you need to tackle sensitive subjects or illustrate complex services, animation can dissect information, captivate audiences and tap into their human emotions. Regardless of the industry your business is in, animation can be a multipurpose investment you can re-use in various sales, marketing or social media campaigns with noticeable ROI.

Let's see how animation can be a simple and highly effective marketing tool in several industries, with a multitude of ways to maximise web traffic, social media growth and business perception.

The benefits of animation on your ROI

Having a video on your homepage makes a website 53% more likely to appear on the first page of Google search results.[17] This is important because the first page of Google captures 71% of clicks (reportedly up to 92% in recent years[18]), with the first five results snapping up 67.6% of all clicks.[19] Google's second page of search results only receives 6% or fewer of all website clicks. This just goes to show how important it is to have a good SEO strategy to get your rankings higher up the page.

Not only is a video appealing, but it can also help to increase credibility and trust from the customer. This is supported by 64% of customers being more likely to buy a product online after watching a video.[20] Real estate listings which include a video receive 403% more enquiries than those without.[21] This mentality isn't just limited to B2C organisations, either, as 96% of B2B organisations use video in their marketing with 73% reporting positive effects on their ROI.[22]

As tempting as it may be, you don't want a full-length feature film explaining your services as 60% of viewers will stop watching within about two minutes,[23] so keep it short and sweet. Animation is the easiest way to convey a complex idea, as the only limits are creativity and budget. While animation can seem like something only Hollywood can afford, it is often a cheaper and more effective way to explain your ideas than an expensive video production with a crew, actors, locations, set and props. Generating images digitally doesn't have the restrictions of reality, either, so an animated explainer video can show literally anything to customers.

To have a successful video and a high ROI, you need to have a goal to begin with. Visualise a clear idea of what the outcome needs to be from the beginning so that the animation will be fit for purpose and have the best effect on your client/intended audience.

A great example is when BlackRock used an interactive video designed to increase 401k contributions – a tax-advantaged retirement account in which people can save some of their income.[24] There was a single goal, and the whole project was designed solely around that one goal. Viewers made choices throughout the video, which essentially showed the financial benefit of contributing to the 401k rather than buying a daily coffee, for example. Although it may sound like a bit of a gimmick, 70% of viewers interacted with the video, with 50% of those who engaged increasing their 401k contributions. Need I say more?

The most integral part of obtaining a high ROI from an animated video is to know what you want the intended outcome to be. With a set goal, the animated video will have a positive effect on sales etc. A good way to incentivise people to watch the entire video is to promise a reward at the end. This can be anything from a fun fact to a voucher, and although it may seem unnecessary, it will make people more likely to watch the whole video and allow the whole message to get across.

How to measure ROI from an animated explainer video

This is entirely dependent on what the goal of the video is and where it is placed (more of that in Chapter 5). Some common goals include increased sales, brand awareness and lead generation. Many companies have specific goals, so your metric will likely be tailored to one specific video. After distinguishing what the goal is, you then need to decide on a metric to measure the success of the video, and in turn the ROI.

Some goals are easier to measure than others, but for sales, you'd be looking at revenue, number of orders etc. Leads are also easy to track, but some other goals, such as brand awareness, are a little trickier. You can incorporate social listening using website analytics to define engagement when you're measuring the success of your brand or company's popularity and gauging current trends in your industry. There are several techniques to acquire data, such as network traffic analysis, ad-hoc applications and web crawling.

Once you've decided how you're going to measure ROI on a shiny new animation, it may be valuable to work out a monetary value, if it's applicable to your goal. This is an easy way to see how much more profit an animation has made you. Sales leads and conversions are the easiest ones to measure as it is simply a process of looking at how much they have increased since you launched your animated video and working out the additional profit.

Animation for specific industries

In every industry, you're faced with many target audiences and competitors. Ideally, you need to find a way of implementing successful strategies to help boost your sales performance. Animation is a simple yet effective tool used by businesses for attracting new clients. It can be a worthwhile long-term investment, flexible not only in sales, but in marketing as well. It captivates viewers, resonating with them for much longer than if they read a blog or article.

If a prospect visits your website and the first thing they're greeted with is an animation, they're likely to stay and watch to fulfil their desire to learn about your services or products.

Marketing in B2B has several challenges, from injecting life into a dull subject to making mathematical equations memorable, cutting through the noise and competition, influencing attitudes towards products and how to present them effectively, and being proactive about generating quality leads. More than any other medium, animation can help marketeers overcome these challenges and reach their goals, enticing and converting their audiences to take a CTA, whether that be more brand awareness, signing up to a newsletter or attending an event.

Animation fits anywhere in your sales funnel and can sell without being salesy. Whether targeting new leads or existing clients, you need to entertain them and show them all the services you offer. An animation can drive good results anywhere on the sales path because it explains something to your audience to educate and entertain them. It need not be a hard sell, but an animation is nonetheless a powerful selling tool, because people learn more effectively when they have fun at the same time.

Let's take a closer look at the role of animation in some specific industries.

Education

It can take as little as 13 milliseconds for the brain to process images, and 40% of nerve fibres are linked to the retina.[25] For any marketeer in the education space, using this medium assures attention, curiosity and retention of complex messages, making it a perfect medium for teaching, learning and retention.

Animation adds a whole new world of flexibility to education and learning. Whether it is for kids, higher education or business training purposes, it allows educators to transfer their teaching to the digital world. Not only is this more accessible for everybody, but the ability to look back at the visuals adds another level of practicality.

People with learning difficulties could greatly benefit from these flexible ways of learning. A study into how animation can be used in higher education found that one of the main benefits is that it facilitates flexible and self-paced learning.[26] This proved successful with individuality and self-assessment.

Presenting information visually, in comparison to written text alone, has shown to improve learning by up to 400% and, on a cognitive level, stimulates the imagination, allowing for faster information processing.[27] Animation can prove a great step forward.

Take a look at www.historybombs.com – an exciting, fun and effective online resource for history teachers to use in the classroom to increase engagement. This is just one great example of how visual learning is being implemented in education, allowing young children to get inspired by the subject. Imagine the limitless possibilities if you used animation for your business education!

The medical field

Animation has significantly benefited the healthcare and pharma industries. Whether you need to tackle sensitive subjects or illustrate 3D medical procedures, animation dissects complex information, captivates audiences and taps into human emotions. Regardless of the health sector your business sits in, animation can be a multipurpose investment you can re-use in various marketing and social media campaigns.

Take Fortis Healthcare as an example. This company have used animation to illustrate medical procedures for its clients to view for many years now. Many of the procedures that Fortis Healthcare offer are life threatening and complex, therefore, being able to convey exactly what happens in these procedures in a professional, sensitive and digestible way is essential for the safety and success of the company.

Using animation to provide in-depth information simply and visually will always be a good investment for the healthcare and pharmaceutical industries, as not only do these videos rack up a lot of views on YouTube but it also protects them from legal action in many areas, thus providing cost avoidance.

In healthcare, you're faced with many target audiences and competitors. Ideally, you need to find a way of implementing a successful and cohesive marketing strategy.

Advertising

Animation for advertising is maybe more B2C than B2B, but they are obviously linked. Interestingly, salamandra.uk responded to a request from the Institute for Practitioners in Advertising last year, asking for data and examples because it wanted to promote animation to its clients.

There are too many examples of animation in advertising using too many styles and approaches to list. The most famous and anticipated annual animation in this field has to be the John Lewis Christmas adverts.

Film and TV titling

From the iconic, memorable and technically impressive to the downright scary, well-designed titling can frame a production, set the tone and create an unforgettable brand. From a technical point of view, title sequences can use any number of techniques. I've highlighted a few here, with some examples.

Typography based. These sequences usually focus on the reveal of the main title and work well with productions which have a distinctive typographic branding, such as Ridley Scott's classic *Alien*.[28] A salamandra.uk studio favourite is *Stranger Things*.[29]

Motion graphics focus mostly on flat shapes and patterns to tell their story. Examples range from titling master Saul Bass, who created some iconic sequences and inspired others like Spielberg's *Catch Me If You Can*,[30] to more abstract or pattern-based titling like the Netflix show *Mozart in the Jungle*.[31]

Illustrative. Title sequences can be an opportunity to explore a different visual style of storytelling to that of the production. For example, *The Incredibles 2*[32] explored a 2D animated style to continue the story, despite the production being a 3D animation. Other productions, such as the *Series Of Unfortunate Events*[33] film from 2004 or Netflix series *Marco Polo*,[34] use intricate and beautifully designed illustrations to re-enforce the tone and setting using a different medium.

3D. In recent years, we have seen a trend towards the use of 3D to create beautiful and often realistic objects with which the camera can interact in an intimate and interesting way. One of the most well-loved examples of this must be the now iconic *Game of Thrones*[35] sequence. The salamandra.uk team love this trend and how it has been employed in different ways in productions such as *Black Sails*,[36] *The Crown*[37] and *Black Panther*[38] (which uses a particularly impressive particle effect).

Film/photography. Simply using elements from the production, be it footage or stills, put together in interesting ways can create effective title sequences. One of the salamandra.uk team's favourite examples of this is *The*

Walking Dead[39] (Season 9) sequence, which uses photographs and footage stitched together so seamlessly, it feels fluid and dynamic. Finally, to end with another studio favourite, the titling for *Anne with an E*[40] is captivating and blends static photographs with footage, 3D and illustrations, resulting in a truly stunning sequence.

Gaming

Gaming is an exciting market for animation that is growing exponentially. At salamandra.uk, we're increasingly asked to help gaming companies with their marketing and animated sizzles, even animating parts of the games themselves.

The video game industry is projected to reach $200 billion by 2023.[41] Whether you're a big player or just starting out in this field, marketing your game correctly is one of the most important factors to consider for any new title.

Game development has become accessible over the last few years, which is probably the core reason why marketing games has become so important. With new games being released every day, it is key to stand out among the noise, sometimes before your game even hits the market. The largest chunk of sales come in the first week,[42] so if nobody knows about the game *until* then… what good is that?

Sharing screenshots of the game/screen recordings can be helpful at showing exactly what the game does, but it's not exciting, enticing or engaging. Having a more creative approach when it comes to making trailers could help overcome all three of these issues. If you want to promote and market your game before it launches (which I highly recommend), then you do not want to post unpolished screenshots which will taint your image for the rest of this process. A bespoke trailer for the release of your game could be the key to success. To get the most out of your game trailers' marketing potential, game studios should not just focus on one platform. YouTube will, of course, see the highest yield as marketers are able to find their target audience easily on the platform but it's not the only platform that will gain a gamer's interest.

Take the company Lightricks as an example. Lightricks decided to home in on Instragram ads. By creating a series of video ads that featured download links, they were able to amass 300,000 app downloads over five days, propelling them to the top of the app chart.[43]

An animation studio can turn your gameplay into thrilling trailers by incorporating the playable characters and promoting a highly visual and exciting piece to your audience. Creating a buzz and showing off the game potential before release, these trailers can be made in the form of animated explainer videos. This approach could produce further hype for the game as giving an idea of its style is an effective way to catch the interest of the viewers. Whether your game is for the app store or console stores, having a trailer video will be more effective than just screenshots, leading to more sales and downloads.[44]

Using animation to create an engaging and enticing trailer can help make an impression by adding another level of storytelling. The first ten seconds matter,[45] so showcasing everything your game has to offer with sleek animations, motion graphics and cinematography is likely to entice the viewer to download it and get involved. First impressions count, so fully immersing users in this way has the potential to impress them straight off the bat.

Another interesting spin-off is that companies like Adverty are creating clever in-game adverts that can be animated. Animated ads on an animated platform? What's not to love?

Summary

Now we've looked at how animation benefits both marketing and sales, provides fantastic value and ROI, and works across a multitude of diverse industries to communicate complex messages, we can clearly see that it is a valuable and highly effective marketing tool.

Target audiences expect to understand what's being sold to them, which is why some businesses are finding new ways of informing and impressing their prospects. By providing content that viewers can learn from, animation swiftly converts into an effective sales tool, whether for B2B or B2C, because viewers can learn about products and services efficiently. And if you use an animation to explain the benefits of your product or service to the user, they are more likely to watch the entire video than read the same content on your website, allowing your message to get across in an engaging way. This makes animation a hugely viable tool in acquiring new prospects or consumers.

Successful businesses strive for simplicity. By explaining things via animation, they can convey complex messages, clarifying misconceptions about the products or services they are selling. Using animation within your marketing and sales strategies incorporates an effective tool that prospects and consumers will appreciate and learn from, raising your chances of a successful sale.

The bottom line is that by making your brand memorable using animation, you create strong images, increase loyalty and generate new and returning customers for business growth and development. From small startups to global multinationals, everyone is relying on these techniques to make their presence felt.

PART TWO
PLAN

When you're considering how to approach your corporate animation project, it helps to understand the three stages to animation: plan, produce and publish (pre-production, production and post-production). Each one segues into the next, so they're all interdependent.

This section will cover the first of these three stages, taking you through all the elements you need to consider, research and decide upon to set the right direction before embarking on the actual animation. The plan (pre-production) phase is a strategic one that looks at your company, competition and industry, as well as ensuring your brand guidelines police your direction, tone of voice, look and feel, the script and the overall storyboard.

Plan is the phase of further developing ideas prior to the actual process of production. This is the time for you and your animation team to take a top-down approach to the project, understanding what it is you want this asset to represent and what reaction you want it to create with your target audiences. In a live-action movie, it is the period before filming starts. In an animation sense, it is the period before any real animating takes place.

As with all great projects, success is in the planning.

chapter 5

A Guide To Business Animation

There are many types of B2B animations, from corporate explainers, presentations, interactive, immersive, training and educational pieces to TV adverts. Each of these requires different steps.

Before you start with any content elements of your animation, you will need to look at the project more strategically and decide on the parameters required. Over and above what you need delivered (eg a ninety-second 2D animation) and understanding your marketing issue, ask yourself why you are doing this. What is the problem or challenge it needs to resolve? In other words, what are the animation's primary objectives and key benefits?

Consider also your positioning, your unique selling point. What is it that differentiates your offering from your competition? What is the one big idea you want your audience to take away from this communication?

When you're planning a B2B animation, it pays to choose a studio that has a tried-and-tested methodology for getting the work done in the most time- and cost-effective way. You don't want an agency or studio that will take a quick brief and go away, decide what they think will work, and then present you with their outcome without any input from you. You need a studio that will collaborate with you throughout the process, getting your sign off at every stage or milestone. That way, there will be no nasty surprises, and you can be secure in the knowledge that you will be delighted with the outcome.

At salamandra.uk, we often get asked how we go about creating an animation. How do we know what is in our clients' heads? This chapter will demystify the animation process and show how a good studio will take its clients along on the journey, making it easy for them, always with the end goal of visually delighting them.

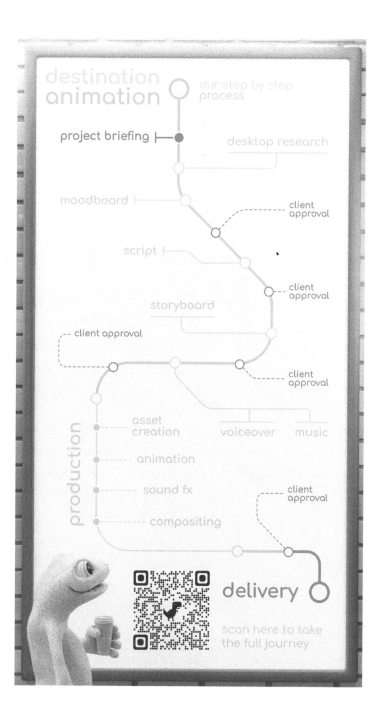

The briefing process

It's important to build a successful relationship with your agency. The briefing process is key, and the best briefs from a client for animated content enable the best work from an animation agency. Writing a good brief and giving helpful collated feedback, being specific and technical (even supplying an industry glossary) in that feedback, makes for a good project foundation.

At salamandra.uk, once we understand that a client has an appetite or need for an animation or a series of animations, the first thing we do is book a briefing session where we ask several questions to ascertain various elements. These form the foundation of the project and ensure that we are going in the right direction to get the best result for our clients.

The most important question your studio should be asking you first and foremost is 'What is your (business) challenge?' The answer will indicate the best path to follow – and it may not even be an animation. Your challenges may range from needing more brand awareness to your target audience needing to understand your product or services or what your business as a whole does. There could be issues with keeping your Zoom or conference participants engaged or getting a complex campaign off the ground.

Whether you run an established company or are just starting out, any or all of these elements could be a daily marketing challenge for your business. Animation could be the solution, but equally, depending on your challenge, a difference approach might be more suitable. Therefore, the briefing process on any project is vital if you are to get the most appropriate outcomes for your challenges. For that reason, make sure you pick an agency or studio that offers a robust briefing tool.

The next questions you want your studio to ask concern the specific brand, product or service you want to promote, why and to whom, because there is always more than one target audience. These audiences could include your end customers, suppliers, internal and external teams, the media and the general public, depending on your industry. Once they have asked all these questions, a good studio team will embark on meaningful desktop research into your brand, your competitors and your industry. No one can convey your message without understanding it first.

Many companies overlook sharing all the services or products they offer with their existing clients, concentrating on those that the client already uses. Your clients will be familiar with the products or services that they already use, but they may be unaware of all the others you offer, so a CTA to help them understand your variety could be all that you require at this stage.

The challenge you need to solve will help determine several things in the animation, such as the tone of voice, the length, the content, direction, script and general approach, and the CTA. For the tone of voice, is your message a serious one? Do you want to come across as professional but approachable, friendly and fun, irreverent and cheeky, serious and sober, traditional, funny or outrageous? The tone will help set what is possible in the visual message and how this will be portrayed.

You then need to establish the length of the animation. An average corporate animation ranges from sixty to ninety seconds, but there are plenty of great thirty second or two+ minute animations, depending on the context. As a general rule of thumb, go shorter for social teasers, TV ads or quick overviews, and longer for training or internal communications, product demos etc.

Typically, viewers only take away two or three messages from your animation, so it's worth distilling what you want included in the piece. Too many messages run the risk that none will be retained. Your studio should ask you during the briefing session to supply the content you would like included in bullet point format in order of preference. The reason for this is that you know your product or service inside out, unlike your studio, whose team is likely just getting to know you and your business.

The bullets allow your studio to pinpoint the most pertinent information and create a strong script précis around this for you. With a typical sixty-second animation, you only have between 70 and 100 words to play with in your voiceover script, allowing for spaces and comfortable pauses. This may seem very few, especially if you think you need to explain a lot about your company products or services, but a good B2B animation studio will be expert at refining your points into an engaging narrative in the script, using the animation and motion graphics to support and expand that narrative and portray the greatest amount of information.

The script can't be waffly; it needs to be succinct, simple, memorable and easy to understand, so your studio must be able to extract the most appropriate elements and weave them into it. It is important that your animation studio team crafts or finesses your script, because they will have in mind how that will translate visually and what transitions are likely. After all, your animation will be your brand's modern-day visual jingle.

The content of your animation will need to reflect what you want to get across, marrying up with the script seamlessly and working with the tone of voice. If you are being serious and sober, you won't want the visual style to be too cartoony or funny looking, for example. It needs to work well with the overall direction of the piece and who you are talking to. Answering your target audience's pain points should be the number one priority in the piece, because that is what will resonate with them and keep them engaged, wanting to know more and re-sharing your animation.

Next, it's important to work out the required CTA for the piece. What do you want your audiences to do once they've viewed it? This should be a key part of the animation and the purpose of the marketing tool that you are creating, because you need to consider what your ROI on this cost to the business will be. Conversion is always the end marketing goal, so what will you pick as the action for your viewer to take?

Once the content is shaped up, the CTA at the end of the piece needs to be clear to make it as easy as possible for your viewer to convert into a customer. This could be as simple as including your contact details: an email address, your website URL or your phone number, or inviting viewers to sign up to your newsletter or attend an event. Or it could be to enter a competition, book a phone call or get further information.

I have seen fantastic corporate animations that don't give any CTA at the end, which is a totally wasted opportunity. This can also be quite frustrating for the viewer, because if they want to know more or follow up, they need to do some research to find you, instead of just having the details at their fingertips. It could be a sale, special offer or campaign you are advertising, so ensure it's easy for the viewer to find and engage with the right elements to take part.

It is key to pinpoint your business challenge at the start of the project to establish the right content, tone of voice, CTA and everything in between before you take any other decision or direction on the animation. This will ensure your animation studio creates the most appropriate piece to give you the best outcomes for your current business and marketing channel.

Desktop research

The next step in the process to create the most effective animation is for your chosen agency's team to conduct some desktop research to ensure they understand your business, competitors and industry landscape. Because you know your business better than they do, they will ask for input from you as part of the briefing process. You may find it is the first time in a while, if ever, that you have looked at the strategic elements of your business and really thought about who your competitors and audiences are. It can be quite a cathartic exercise.

Your studio team will google your brands, and your competitors', comparing their content, look and feel, tone of voice etc with the plans for your animation. This research can bring up several elements. For example, if there is a lot of uniformity in the look and feel, content and tone of voice in your industry, a few changes and tweaks to your message can really make you stand out in the crowd and engage with your audience.

CASE STUDY – MILLWOOD SERVICING LTD

When salamandra.uk was approached by Millwood Servicing Ltd, a fire-safety services company, to rebrand its image, we were given the task of providing messaging and brand guidelines, including creating an animation to act as a corporate explainer. The aim of rebranding Millwood Servicing was to refresh its outdated look and engage potential clients in a noisy and highly competitive market, increasing its online brand awareness to generate new leads.

In a market that traditionally builds on the fear of what might happen in a fire, Millwood's approach was focused on prevention, safeguarding and being a family-run business that cares for its staff and clients. After gaining an understanding on the topic of fire-safety services through a commissioned messaging workshop with the client, we were able to distil the Millwood story into a comprehensive document that detailed the company messaging and brand guidelines.

Using the messaging and branding, we created an informative one-minute corporate explainer animation to educate potential customers on the products and services Millwood offers. The secondary aims were to generate new leads and increase the company's online brand awareness. The animation had a completely fresh approach, which was clean and modern, and incorporated a consistent image with the animation in line with the brand guidelines we'd created. The animated characters reflected a stylised version of the owner, his family and members of his team to underline the family feel of the company.

The focus was on safeguarding, prevention, security and family heritage as opposed to fear, frights, terror and alarm. This has helped Millwood stand out head and shoulders above its competition, and its rapid turnover growth has reflected this.

It's vital to explain your industry in your brief to your studio, because each sector has its own type of language and approach that is familiar to those within it.

To resonate and engage with a particular group, you need to incorporate some familiar elements in your animation to create trust, familiarity and acceptance. It may be the first time you, particularly if you are a business owner, have experienced the creative part of a project and been key to its development. This is great fun, like being taken to a candy shop and allowed to pick what you fancy from all that is on offer.

This exercise helps your studio team to shape the visual content, and then use their skills to create just the right look and feel for your brand and business. Without this important step, your project could be created on the whim of your studio team. It's the best way to ensure that from the start, your piece will resonate memorably with your chosen target market. After all, you want to give your competitors a run for their money, and you need to ensure that every marketing penny you spend is used as profitably as possible. What better way to lay down these foundations than with the right groundwork research to ensure client engagement, and excitement, from the start?

Where to start

Clients often ask the salamandra.uk team how we get their animations so right, almost as if we can see inside their heads. The answer is that we are robust in preparing the foundations with our briefing and ensure we ask the right questions at the start.

Target audience

Understanding your budget is important to gauge what length and complexity of animation is possible within your financial scope. To maximise ROI, you need to help your studio understand who your animation will be addressing, because that will shape everything about your piece, from the script, to the content and tone of voice. You need to define your target audience or audiences, uncovering their perceptions or misconceptions about your product or service. What is their demographic: their sex, age, income, geographic location, socio-economic status etc? You'll also need to know their psychographics, such as price sensitivity, quality perceptions, attitudes and emotions surrounding your brand and offering.

Your internal audience includes:

o All your current staff from each department.

o Any potential or future employees you may want to attract into the business.

o Your various internal departments such as HR (think induction and attracting the right calibre of candidate who can buy into what the company does), sales, marketing/PR (messaging and advertising), finance and distribution. Every member of staff is a potential brand ambassador, so your sales and marketing department is potentially the total number of staff you have.

Your external audience includes:

o   Existing clients on your books.

o   Past clients whose interest you can rekindle.

o   Potential clients that you'd like to convert.

o   Your competition, which might include some potential future employees.

o   Your current and future sponsors or investors. This group is particularly relevant when you're organising events, either online or in person.

o   Charities that you support or those that may want your support. Your animation can help to see if your combined core values align.

o   Suppliers (accountants, software suppliers, banks, plumbers etc).

o   The general public building brand goodwill for your company, which translates to an improved bottom line.

Starting from the top, your current staff are your best ambassadors in the field and can be your secret weapon when it comes to evangelising your company. The better they can articulate what you do, the better they can advertise your company or business for you. And like social media influencers, your internal team has the right believability and/or gravitas because they are at the 'coal face' of your business, privy to all its inner workings, systems, culture and values.

If your animation is a corporate explainer that outlines what your business does, including all your services, succinctly and memorably, then what better way is there to inform your team? And as they will all then be 'singing from the same song sheet', your messaging about the business will be joined up into a uniform 'elevator pitch' across your whole staff.

Attracting the right staff is crucial to any ambitious business. Creating an environment with an organic 'people-pull' because potential candidates are taken with what you do makes recruiting easy. Because these candidates have seen your corporate explainer online, and have liked what they've seen, they will already be 'sold' about working with you. And for future or new employees, your animation makes a wonderful induction tool.

Internal departments are an important audience that will capitalise on understanding and using your explainer video asset. The obvious one is sales, because your animation is a fantastic sales asset that can be repurposed in many ways on many platforms. Marketing and PR are also departments that will be using this asset, online and in print, in advertising and as part of the marketing narrative. Your finance department needs to approve the spend for your animation project, so they need to feel vindicated when watching the end result. Their happiness and pride in their decision will add them to your team of brand evangelists.

Existing clients are familiar with the products or services they buy from you, but they may not know about all the others your company offers. Your corporate animation asset will highlight these to your clients, often bringing about a lightbulb moment when they exclaim, 'Oh, I didn't know you also did that!' Upselling to an existing client? What's not to like?

Potential clients are still learning about you, whether they're checking out your website or online presence, attending a sales meeting or interacting with your staff. An animation tool that engages with them because it identifies and answers their pain points is a powerful asset in converting sales, and it's one they can share with family, friends and colleagues.

Your competitors are likely to be checking your business out online or via anecdotal information gathered in the marketplace. They will use your animation asset to benchmark your company and see whether you are a threat or not, and where in the pecking order you sit. With a good explainer video, there's a high chance you'll be way ahead of them, rather than equals or behind them.

Investors are a vital audience if you are growing the business and need financial support to do this. Convincing them with your joined-up thinking in an animated explainer will likely win them over before you even start with your pitch. They will grasp the concept and buy into it more easily if they understand what you do.

The animation can be a great tool if you are supporting a charity event, as it or its URL can be used as part of the marketing campaign. And what better way to attract the best people to work with – and the attention of the general public – than to have your ambassador animation front and centre of all you company's communications?

CASE STUDY – ROYAL ALBERT HALL

The Royal Albert Hall (the Hall) team recognised that its iconic round building can be confusing to its various audiences, from ticket purchasers, to artists, suppliers and staff. They wanted an animated tool that would quickly and simply illustrate the layout of the building, which looks the same whichever entrance you take.

Amazingly, the Hall did not have up to date building blueprints for us to base our drawings on, which meant we needed to site visit to photograph and hand draw every floor to create the interactive architectural 3D piece. Our art director, known to be a little accident prone, was on the top floor (having been given all access permissions), sketching the domed section among a lot of cabling and equipment. A security guard quizzed her about being up there, and then informed her that the entire floor was set up for that evening's performance by the iconic *Cirque du Soleil*. All those cables around her were in fact pyrotechnics!

We do like to create fireworks for our clients, but not in the literal sense...

We were commissioned to create an interactive map and seating plan of this iconic London venue. After drawing out each floor, we emulated the sketches to design the floors in 3D software, which was then rendered out as full 3D architectural-style images. We designed and added the different elements to each floor, giving a description to the icons, including the Hall's range of restaurants, bars and facilities. Originally, the Hall had a flat non-interactive 2D map, but its team wanted an interactive version that would demystify the space and allow the user to comprehend where the different facilities are located throughout the Hall with a clickable function for more information.

After completing the design and rendering, and adding the colour and detail, we coded the whole map so that each floor of the building could be stacked one on top of another, as well as deconstructed to display each floor separately, with the inclusion of all the interactive information on the various facilities. You can take a look at our work here: www.royalalberthall.com/plan-your-visit-essential-safety-information/venue-and-seating-plan/venue-plan

We loved learning about the building and seeing the positive client reaction when the Hall team first saw the completed project. It was rewarding to see it coming together as the interaction took shape, and it is still helping the Royal Albert Hall's target audiences find their way around.

Your why

To get the right resonance, gravitas and content in your project, your studio will need to understand your why for several elements, starting with your company purpose. Why does your company exist? What do you bring to your customers and audiences? Understanding this will help distil your core elements and *raison d'être*.

Next will be details of your company brand, guidelines and core values. Again, this will help your studio identify what is important to you and your brand, and what is moveable and immovable with regards to messaging and visuals.

You need to have an idea of where you want your animation to end up. Although your studio will no doubt expand on your original thoughts, it's important that you have an idea upfront to help guide the direction and find ways to repurpose the work. The outcomes you are expecting are also important to know, as well as an idea of a budget, because essentially this will shape what is possible and impossible within those parameters.

Your tone of voice

This brings us to tone of voice – how do you want your customers to perceive you? For example, should your brand come across as serious, business oriented and professional, friendly, or irreverent and off the wall? Young or experienced, hipster or traditional? It's important to consider what related marketing activities you or your competitors have done previously, which may have been seen by your target audience and affect your project.

The tone of voice can be led by your brand guidelines. They will make clear any parameters to work within (or avoid) in the scope of your animation project. Most corporates opt for a professional feel, but still want to keep it human and approachable. Think H2H instead of B2B.

Getting the tone of voice right for your animation is key to the success of the project.

Summary

Good foundations are vital in any creative process or endeavour, not least for an animation project. Starting with a robust briefing session where your studio team will ask you pertinent questions will allow them to do some background research on your business and industry to frame the approach to be taken. This will help them grasp the identity of your target audiences, how to speak to them, and the parameters aligned with your brand to convey your complex messages. The end goal is always to create something which engages your audience to take the required CTA to achieve your marketing and branding goals.

Now we have established the whys and wherefores of building your B2B animation, let's delve into preparing for the actual content of the piece.

chapter 6

Mood

This chapter will be covering the initial creative stages in pre-production, establishing the particulars of the narrative and direction, and getting buy-in from stakeholders as to how the final product will feel, look and sound. By focusing on the mood board, script and storyboard, you'll nail the visible and audible content before going into production and the actual animating, which is the costly section.

Mood board

The first 'creative' piece your studio will put together for you is a mood board. This entails combining elements of other animations and design on to a page like a static scrapbook, showing lots of different styles and approaches, colour schemes, fonts and content for you to choose from.

The idea is that you and your team look at the mood board that has been created specifically for your company and industry, with elements that have been identified as appropriate for your brand and that will resonate with your target audience. You then let the studio team know what you like and what you don't. For example, you may say that you love this colour scheme, character design and element, but can they mix them with that style and these other elements. This way, the studio team can start to see what is in your head and pick out what resonates with you and your team to help them shape the look and feel of the piece.

It's usually a fun experience which will get you excited as you become an essential part of the process. Ideally, you'll be taken on the journey with your studio team. Make sure they ask you to sign off every milestone in a collaborate way.

Script

From the perspective of producing a sixty-second explainer animation for B2B marketing, you need a crisp, succinct, easy-to-understand and engaging script, because the best animation videos are the ones that really capture the imagination. Although you might think the moving elements are the most important parts of an animation, visuals are only half of what makes an explainer video effective. The other half is the sound and script (and the voiceover, should it be used) in the explainer. These elements play a pivotal role. The visuals reinforce what is being explained, but the script is key. It holds many of your messages, so it needs to be easy to understand.

Due to the economy of words, all fat needs to be trimmed so the script is on point. It will accompany the storyboard, which is a cartoon-style strip that helps to sketch out what will be happening in the animation in each scene, along with what part of the script it covers.

Give your studio team bullet points of the content you would like your animation to cover in order of preference. Then the team can wordsmith a script around two or a maximum of three key messages. Any more messages and none are likely to be remembered by the viewer. The script needs to make sense to the viewer with no additional context.

The script and the storyboard (more on that later in the chapter) need to encompass the context of the piece, which may include the story background and outline one or two core marketing messages. The story will identify your target customer – the one with the problem, pain point or challenge that your product or service solves. It can also explain the problem that your solution fixes and what happens if your target customer does nothing instead. You need to outline some of the typical buying-cycle questions or objections, and have a creative concept and environment that ties all this messaging together. And the story can show the marvellous results customers can expect after they have used or implemented your product or service.

The focus would change for other types of animations, such as an educational animation explaining how to use a product, or training or internal HR animations, or one delving into a product's technical specifications. But the common point is that you need clarity in the script due to the lack of words to present the idea within sixty seconds. Keep it brief and simple. The job of the animation is to pique the interest of your viewers to find out more, communicate your value and motivate them to take the next step in the sale cycle.

Because voice and images will be working in tandem, your studio team will need to decide which parts of the story work best delivered as voiceover narration or character dialogue, which work best in motion graphics or animation, and which work best in text to emphasise a point or when you can't convey that piece of information with other media. They will need to make sure that each medium complements the others with none overlapping and repeating the same information, but rather expanding on the message while compressing the time needed to convey it.

The most important element to make this asset a useful marketing and sales tool is the CTA. Ensure that you tell your audience what to do next, whether that be to share the information, go to a URL, click and fill in a form or contact your sales team. At the very least, include your website details at the end so they can find out more.

Voiceover

Should you decide to use one, your voiceover needs to be a considered choice. Unless you are doing a customer case study, or featuring a nonprofit or charity where it makes sense to use an actual customer's voice, I would highly recommend using a professional voiceover artist.

While your budget may not stretch to someone famous such as Joanna Lumley, who has one of the most recognised voices in the UK, your professional voiceover artist can adapt and emulate many styles. With your input, your studio will be able to advise on whether your target audience would benefit from a male, female or child's voice, and whether your animation would resonate better with a regional accent or received pronunciation. The tone for the piece will set the scene for the voiceover artist.

Access to the right level of studio equipment and technology is vital to achieve the quality of sound required for your animation. Voiceover artists are professional actors and performers who can often emulate any accent, while working with studio recording equipment and sound engineers to ensure the highest quality sound output. Voiceovers can also be recorded in any international language should your business need this.

These professional artists are also adept at successfully taking a client brief and understanding the requirements from a business perspective, including respecting your time and communication preferences. They will get the job done right and quickly, saving you time and money by only needing one or two takes. An inexperienced person will take many more and probably still not sound as good, although there are always exceptions, as you will see in the case study coming up. They will give you feedback and direction, because actors understand diction, inflection, cadence, tone, emphasis and pitch, and they will often give you a couple of takes that can be used for editing purposes down the line.

Professional voiceover artists build trust in your brand because the quality and authority in their narration can influence your end audience. You want the animation to resonate with your target audience, and the voice (or voices) delivering your message is a key component.

CASE STUDY – TEENIE TOTS

This case study is a good example of the exception to the rule when it comes to deciding on a professional voiceover artist versus the client representing themselves.

The owner of Teenie Tots Childminding has a passion for working with and taking care of children in her hometown of Kirriemuir, Scotland. The salamandra.uk team tried using a voiceover artist for her animated children's book, but once the owner sent a sample of her reading her own story, we were so enchanted with how natural and engaging it sounded that we decided to use her in place of the voiceover artist. After years of telling stories to her little wards, she could inject just the right intonation and emphasis throughout the animation to bring the audience along with her. As she had written it herself, she had a personal connection to the story.

The book contained lots of appealing onomatopoeia, which meant we could have fun animating the sounds and syncing these with the animation and effects in the scene. The coupling of sound and vision is a great medium for communicating to children in a way that will hold their attention, help them to understand what is being said and make the learning process seem less formal than being told something by adults, which can be stressful for them.

The resultant voiceover comes from the heart and provides a warm and authentic feel to the story. We were then able to put the story in motion, and we could not be more pleased with the beautiful, endearing and quirky outcome. You can take a look at www.salamandra. uk/our-work/teenietots

We at salamandra.uk love working on kids' content. It allows us to speak to our inner child.

Storyboard

This is a vital stage that can make or break an animation as it is where a lot of the biggest creative decisions are made. Here, your studio team takes the abstract concepts described in the script and finds creative ways to represent them visually.

While the fine details of the visuals are not defined in the storyboard, the team starts to block out the style in terms of characters, setting and iconography. Any visual languages and metaphors that tell the story will be conceptualised at this point, and motion graphics and on-screen text will be included for approval by you, the client.

Your studio team will make decisions at this stage regarding how the animation will flow and the feel of the pacing – will the camera move through the content, or will the content morph and shift in front of the camera? How will the scenes transition? Will the animation style be fluid and smooth, or bouncy, or with cuts and big impacts?

Technically, the storyboard serves as the reference point for the illustrators (2D) or modellers and riggers (3D – more on riggers in Chapter 7) to work from when they're creating everything needed for the animation. It also acts as the guide for the animators to work to.

A storyboard looks like a cartoon strip and is essentially a series of drawings based on the script which is used as a visual guide throughout the rest of the animation production. It will include a sequence of roughly drawn scenes to tell the story, outlining whatever the viewer will hear or see on screen and all the technical information for each scene. This process requires planning, production and revision by your studio before it is approved by you and your team.

The storyboard will be the framework for the narrative. Your studio team will work around the voice recording to time the action of the animation so they match together perfectly, ensuring it all flows and has a beginning, middle and end. This helps the animators to work out how much time they have for every transition or 'cartoon square' in the storyboard, action shot or background pan to enable the narrative to unfold seamlessly in a joined-up way.

The storyboard's primary goal is to convey the story visually and via script to look as close as possible to the intention of the final animation. By seeing it, you can understand straight away what is going on in the story. More importantly, making changes is much easier and cheaper on a storyboard compared to a finished animation. An approved storyboard acts as a reference for the rest of the project, bridging the gap between the script and the final animation and getting everyone on the same page. If used properly, it avoids flaws and keeps things on track and within budget.

Summary

To set the required mood for your animation and finish the plan (pre-production) part, you need to identify the right tone within the constraints of your brand guidelines. With the help of your studio wordsmith, you'll create a concise and engaging script that encompasses the messages you need to get across succinctly, illustrated by a cartoon-strip storyboard to give you an overall picture of what will happen in your animation, both visually and audibly. The choice of voiceover talent and using professional equipment for the recording is key to a successful and memorable animation that can become the marketing asset you have anticipated.

This section and all its elements need to be signed off before the produce (production) stage starts – ostensibly, the most expensive part of the process. It is in your interests to get all the groundwork done and agreed before moving on to production to ensure the project does not need to go back a few expensive steps down the line.

PART THREE

PRODUCE

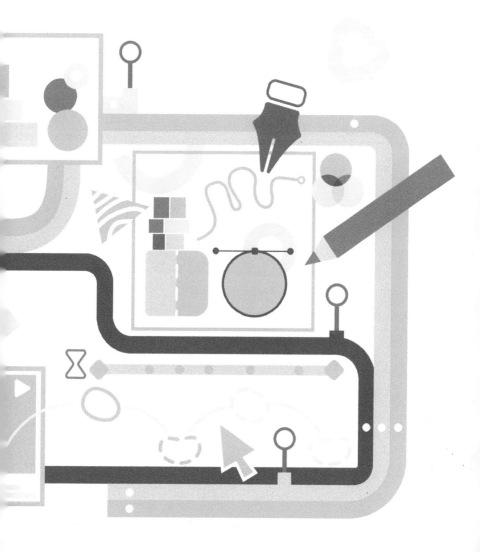

The produce (production) part is the second of our three Ps process. It is the path by which an animated film goes from a creator's brain to the screen for the world to see. Understanding all the elements of this stage is vital in taking the first step to creating your own vision.

This section includes the visuals, animatic, asset design and creation, and the animation itself, be it two dimensional, three-dimensional using AR, VR or a mixture of each.

Q **chapter 7**

Visuals

The produce part of the project is where the magic happens and all the ideas on paper turn into an animated reality – or fantasy, depending on your required look, feel and content. The visuals come together with an animatic, the environment and asset design, followed by the motion graphics and the animations themselves, whether they're in 2D, 3D, stop motion, AR or VR, or mixed up with film footage. This is the costliest part of the animation project because it requires the expert animators to hone their skills to the brief's requirements and timelines.

In a live-action video, whatever is filmed already exists in the real world – the sun, the background, the environment and the people, along with the sounds, voices, effects etc. To create the shoot, you need camera and sound people, stylists, actors, venue and the right lighting or time of the day.

When animating, you need to create every element, from colour to lighting, the characters, their fluid movement, the foley[46]/sound effects, music, emotion, tone and energy. It can take a group of people four to six weeks to create a professional sixty-second animation, including client approvals throughout, which is why the cost of an animation can be quite high.

Let's look at the creation of the visuals in more detail.

Animatic

Once your script and storyboard are done and your voiceover(s) recorded, depending on the complexity of the animation, it's time to create the animatic. This is a loose version of what your final piece will look like in motion.

This exercise is primarily for the in-house studio team and is rarely shared with you. Basically, the storyboard is cut up and timed with the voiceover so the team can work out how many seconds each section is allowed, helping them with the animation process. The reason it's not shown to you is that the animatic looks nothing like the end piece; it simply aids the studio with the timing of each sector and working out the flow of each second of animation to tie in with the narrative and voiceover. Because studios are used to working with these rough tools and you are (most likely) not, you might get a fright if you see this simplistic, almost childish exercise which has no proper flow, animation or polish.

Rest assured, this is *not* how your animation will look and feel. If you wish, you can always have a look once you have approved the final animation to see the journey of your asset and what is involved in putting your vision into animation. This is a super-valuable exercise for students of animation to grasp the requirements of timing and content combined.

An animatic is particularly important for a longer animation, such as a training or educational piece where an error in timing will affect the development and narration of the rest of the piece. Its purpose is to ensure the correct timing, helping your studio team with figuring out smooth transitions and how the voiceover will work with the motion.

Style frame

Once you have signed off the look and feel, and reviewed and chosen various styles of animation or designs with the mood-board exercise, it is time for the creatives to start creating your tailored animation world.

When designing all the assets for this process, the creatives will produce a style frame for the studio team to follow. This will outline the colour palette, and the look and feel of the overall story, which could be abstract, modern, vintage, detailed and painterly or photorealistic. All the assets will need to match the style frame, including character design if there are any included.

Some studios use re-usable templated assets to pop-
ulate your animation quickly and cheaply. This is cost
effective, but your vision is limited to the templates
available, so it will make your asset less unique. This
approach can also be obvious to anyone used to viewing
animations.

Bespoke assets can have positive tangible benefits
because they are designed specifically for you and your
target audience, and created around your brand guidelines. This will exponentially improve your brand asset
as the designed elements will couch and enhance your
message. If characters are included, your studio team
will develop an approach and put some designs together
for your approval. When creating the animation portion,
they will give you a flavour of where they are going with
this by sharing snippets for your approval and sign off.

Some of these elements may be designed by several
animators concurrently, so along with communication
between them, the style frame is vital so that the look,
feel and direction of the storyboard remain uniform and
joined up. This way, every element will look like it belongs
to the piece, rather than disparate or out of place.

When there are several characters to be designed, the
style frame will include one or two examples to denote
how they might look. It may also include a specific
approach to animating each character, such as whether
there is a lot of bounce to their movement, or it is more
staccato or natural and film-like.

The style frame will help your animation team create the complete variety of assets to be animated, such as drawing an office fountain pen or a fluffy cloud, and everything in between. This is a fun part of the process as elements start coming to life and you can get a glimpse of what the final animation will look like. What was only part of a 'cartoon' strip storyboard jumps out of its confines and takes shape visually as the process progresses.

CASE STUDY – NET CS

A good example of how creating to a style frame to enable various animators to work together is vital for a joined-up piece is a project salamandra.uk did for NET CS.

This business works around telecommunications, installing internet and mobile antennas into or on church steeples up and down the UK. Its team approached us as they wanted something to communicate quickly, succinctly and in an easy-to-understand manner how this can be done in an unobtrusive and architecturally sensitive way for often listed buildings. Their intention was to get the buy-in from the parish administrators.

As NET CS's target audience is diverse, our studio creatives had to come up with a diverse set of characters to portray this. For them to do this successfully, the style frame had to reflect all the requirements, direction and parameters clearly and visually so that any creative in the studio could pick up the project and stay within the brief.

The result was a joined-up animation with a rich variety of matching characters and assets that clearly
explained the service and all its benefits. Watching
the finished animation, you would never think it was
done by various individual creatives, all with their
own unique styles, as the look and feel is seamless
and uniform throughout.

Check it out here: www.salamandra.uk/our-work/netcs1

Asset design and creation

Each scene or panel of the storyboard needs to be created, whether that means designing a countryside scene
or office interior. The former may include, for example,

mountains and valleys, grass, sheep on the hill and a tractor. Your studio team will decide which elements will need to be animated and plan accordingly. And like a film shoot, the animators need to decide which angles the camera will take and design the elements according-ly. For example, is the countryside being panned across? Is the office seen from a top-down perspective? Where is the light coming from?

The camera angles and lighting requirements will be shaped by the storyboard, but your studio team will need to fine tune and tweak how these work once the creation of the assets starts and, more importantly, the transitions are created between each 'scene' or sto-ryboard 'cartoon' strip. When your animation is in 2D, from a lighting perspective, it's important to consider the time of day. This will be dictated by the elements of the narrative, such as the colours, shadows and feel of scene, which will need to match this element. In 3D, the lighting and time of day would be established after building and texturing the assets, as placing lights on to a 3D scene will affect and change the look of the objects, just like in real life.

Sometimes, you might already have assets in another format, such as a book or printed material, and need to repurpose these and turn them into or include them in an animation. This process involves redrawing the elements, if layered files are not available, into the software required to enable the animators to do their magic when adding motion.

In 2D animation, after your studio team has established the style frame, every object needs to be illustrated by designers in such a way that it can be cut up for animation. Where objects are seen from multiple angles, they will need to be drawn multiple times, as you can't move a camera around a 2D illustration. Fortunately, studios have some clever trickery.

There are several approaches to 2D asset creation, depending on the style of animation. In 2D vector style or motion graphics, most often used in explainer videos, the assets tend to be created by layering flat shapes together using software like Illustrator, before being cut up and layered for animation. Alternatively, in hand-drawn animation, all the assets have to be redrawn for every frame (at twenty-five frames a second – that is why this technique is so time consuming).

For 3D asset creation, there's a different process, which can be a lot more involved. While in 2D, your studio team draws up assets in the colours and lighting they will be shown in during the animation, in 3D, they build the asset as a plain three-dimensional object first, known as modelling. Within modelling, there are a lot of complex techniques, as the team creates what is known as a mesh.

Imagine a cube – it has six sides, each of which is a flat square (known as a face) with joining points at each corner (known as vertices). All objects made in 3D are just built up of more complex versions of this idea. The job of the modeller is to create a series of faces (usually square or triangular), joined up with vertices at the corners, but when they're building a photorealistic product model, for example, it's quite common to get up to hundreds or thousands of faces.

Once the models are created, they go into texturing – this means applying 'materials' to the plain model. It's a bit like painting the surface of the model, only the studio team has to create the paint by combining colour with other properties like how shiny, bumpy or translucent the surface should be.

Once the team has textured your objects or characters, these might need rigging. Rigging is the process of adding 'bones' into the model, so that parts of it can be animated to move independently of each other. Although most often used in characters, giving them a skeleton (or armature) to animate human movement, rigging is also used in objects to control movement. For example, your studio team might rig a book so that it can be opened and the pages can turn.

Finally, once all the assets for a scene are modelled, textured and rigged if needed, they can be arranged into the 3D environment, where your studio team can move the camera around and view them from all angles without having to redraw or recreate the assets. In 2D, lighting is done as part of the asset creation, but in 3D, this is usually done after animating the scene (before setting it to render) so your team has a better idea of where the camera will be looking.

Motion

Motion is where the magic really happens. This is the time when all the elements and assets come to life. The mood board, the script, the voiceover, the animatic and all the designed assets come together to inspire the movement.

You and your studio team will make the decision on the type of animation during the briefing stage at the start of the process, and each stage after that (eg mood board, storyboard, script, assets etc) is defined by that decision. The animation approach needs to be decided upfront because it affects every element up to this point, including timings and costs. How you are likely to use this asset going forwards, or what marketing purpose and messaging tone you need it for in the first instance, will affect the animation type your studio will recommend.

Animating

The process of animating runs through how the assets are taken into motion, following the outline in the storyboard and pacing it to the music and voiceover. Animators start by defining distinct sections of animation that take place in the same environment or within a continuous sequence of actions, known as scenes, just like in live-action film. For each scene, the animators will create the intended motion with the illustrated assets, working to the pacing established in the voiceover.

These scenes will each need to be blended from one to the next with a 'transition', which can range from a simple cut or wipe, through to a complex and abstract morphing of one scene's elements to the next.

Motion is created through a series of frames played one after another. Generally, animations run at twenty-four to thirty frames per second, depending on how they are made, so a six-second scene in an animation would need around 150 frames.

The way your animators create this motion will differ slightly depending on the animation style, but at the core of all styles of animation is the process of determining the key poses, creating the movement between them, then threading each pose together to form the action.

Imagine an animation of a bouncing ball. In this instance, the core poses would be the ball at the highest point and when it hits the floor. If you just toggled between the two key poses, also known as 'keyframes', you would get the sense that the ball was teleporting between the two points rather than bouncing. For an animator to make this motion look convincing, they need to add 'in-between frames'. The more in-between frames they add, the longer the movement takes when it's played back.

In hand-drawn animation, this process is known as 'inbetweening'. Of course, every one of these in-between frames needs to be drawn in by hand, which is why it is a complex and time-intensive process. For digital animation techniques, most often used in B2B animations, such as 2D vector-based, motion graphics or 3D animation, this process is called interpolation, and requires the use and understanding of complex animation software, often along with a lot of manual tweaking and polishing.

With the wider picture of creating a full animation, keyframes and the motion in between them must be individually applied to every object or element in the scene that is moving. This is pretty involved, especially as scenes get more complex, with potentially hundreds of moving elements that must be animated. Especially complex is animating organic elements, like characters, firstly because they tend to have a lot of moving parts, and secondly, because people are wired to notice when the animation of living things, especially humans, doesn't quite look right.

Now you have a basic understanding of the principle and theory of animation, let's run through a few terms and suggestions that your animation studio team might use when they're discussing the way they are animating. It is helpful to understand how these impact your animation.

When creating your animation, your animators may refer to the fluidity of movement, discussing how the animation should feel – for example, smooth or bouncy? The term 'easing' is a measure of how much time elements will take to accelerate and slow down. When an object moves from A to B at a constant rate, this is called a linear movement, which often looks flat and uninteresting. But if it is 'eased', depending on where the acceleration and slowing is applied to the movement, it can feel slick, bouncy, smooth or fluid. Your animators can create different feels to the movement of the objects, thereby creating different emotions in your audiences.

One of the most important factors to understand is how your studio will need to animate differently depending on whether they are working in 2D or 3D. In 2D, when the assets are created in two dimensions, they cannot be animated by turning, only by moving or rotating them in two directions. Here, the animators will focus on animating elements on and off in an engaging way, or animating movements in elements or characters within an illustrated scene from a pre-established angle.

In 3D animation, the assets themselves are created as three-dimensional objects and placed into an environment within the animation software. The animators will place a camera and lighting into this scene, so they can 'look through' and move around the camera to see different angles on the assets. The camera movement can be keyframed in, just like any other asset.

This element of camera animation, allowing animators to act like a director of photography on a film set, is one of the key differences between animating in 2D and 3D. Rather than just animating the assets in the scene, which animators can now do across three directions rather than two, they need to consider how the camera will move around the scene and interact with the objects, which can have a major effect on the feel of the animation. Does the camera convey an inspiring emotion with big sweeping motions, or a sense of threat and unwanted observation, based on where it is viewing the scene? A camera angle might be used below a product to create a sense of impressiveness for the viewer, or at eye level to make the viewer feel they are part of a scenario.

No matter the technique – hand drawn, 2D or 3D – creating movement is all about conveying and instilling emotion. We as humans are hardwired to respond to movement emotionally – be that associating bounciness with happiness, slow, sluggish movement with sadness or boredom, or interpreting sharp bursts or jagged movement as threatening. The role of an animator is to convey the emotion that you need your audiences to feel through the way that an object, character or camera moves.

Lighting

Lighting is an important aspect of any animation project, particularly in 3D. This is the process in which the light sources of the environment – including shades, shadows and reflections – are created. Animation lighting is like photography or film with their combination of light sources to either draw attention to a special part of the setting, set the overall mood of the scene or represent natural properties such as the time of day, the weather or even the season.

In 3D, lighting can be even more significant in adverts, product visualisations or hyperrealistic animations. Applied correctly, the lighting can significantly bring out various details of the objects. And to be honest, everything just looks unappealing and flat without the right lighting.

Real-world light around us is a complex combination of ambient and additional light sources. Most of the light we see illuminates our sky and bounces countless times in the environment. Rendering engines can create similar effects by adding a lighting value to all the pixels in the image, and there are various types of light, including directional light, point light, area light and spotlight.

The most common techniques used in animation are:

o **Three-point lighting.** The first light is the key light – the most intense and primary source of light from one side of the subject. The second light is the fill-in light – less intense, it's placed on the other side to fill in the shadows cast from the first light. The third light is the rim light – placed behind the object to separate it from the background.

o **Two-point lighting.** This is like what we see in real life, which is a primary source of light – the sunlight – and a second light surrounding it – the sky's ambient lighting.

o **One-point lighting.** Only one light source
makes for an extreme and dramatic effect,
like a theatre spotlight.

Summary

Like a major motion picture, when you're preparing for
your animation, every element needs to be in place before the camera starts to roll. Or, in our case, before the
animation starts. That will include setting up the lighting,
the props, the background or backdrop, the characters,
their outfits and look. The only thing that can be added
later, much like a film set, are any recorded sounds, as
well as editing and tweaking the colour calibration and
definition.

The assets to dress your animation, outlined after the
storyboard is approved, need to be created and ticked
off before your studio moves on to the next section. Your
studio team will consider how the transitions will work
from scene to scene and how the assets will be required
to look and move to represent that narrative. The look and
feel will need to follow the agreed style frame, and each
sector of your storyboard will be worked on to ensure all
elements are ready for the next stage.

It's often during this phase that the studio creatives will start to formulate how the actual animation will work to represent what is happening in the narrative.

PART FOUR
PUBLISH

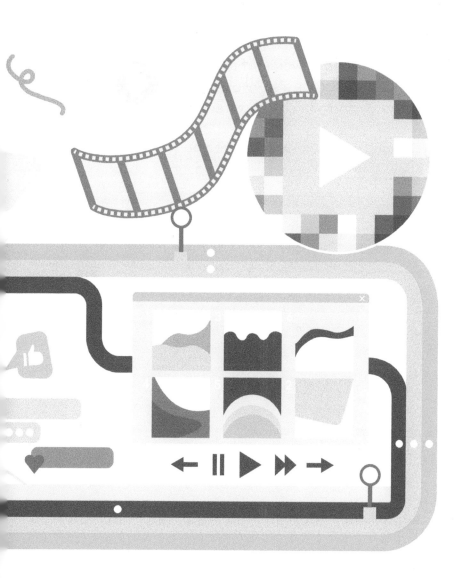

Here we are at the last section of your journey to *Destination Animation*. Publish involves exporting or rendering out the animation frames, and then editing the pieces of animation together using video editing software. The already integrated soundtrack and the added sound effects are combined during the final edit.

In this part, I'll cover all the elements that happen once the animating movement has been created and approved by you. This stage also involves further processes such as compositing and colour correction.

Finally, we will look at where you will share your lovely new animation once it is created.

chapter 8

The Technical Elements

There are certain technical elements that are essential to making sure your animation asset will be an immersive and engaging experience for your target audience. Your chosen studio team will, of course, be familiar with all these elements, but here's an outline of the most important.

Sound effects and music

Let's return to the analogy of your animation being a visual jingle. The sound element is often underestimated in importance, but it makes up an equal part of the rich tapestry of putting together an animation.

Sound is important because it engages your audience and helps to deliver the information and tone of your animation, thereby increasing the value of the asset. It evokes an emotional response, supporting and emphasising what your audiences will see, setting a mood for them to experience. If a jarring piece of music or sound effect does not align with your messaging or target audience, it can undo all the creative aspects of other sectors of the animation. Just think how people's reaction to sound has been responsible for the rise and success of audio business platforms such as Clubhouse, for example.

When used well, language, sound effects, music and even silence can take your animation to the next level as a complete audience experience. Sound needs to support and be timed to every visual and shot, rather than left as an afterthought.

Sound can be enormous fun. Your animation will be elevated by a few carefully selected sound effects to support your narrative, such as the 'ping' of a lift, the tap-tap of someone typing on a laptop or water dripping. Imaging these elements in silence with just the visuals, and then imagine them with the right sound effects. It's quite a transformative experience. Sound places your audience in the narrative. Your animation sound specialists can pick abstract sounds to support the bounce of an object or a swoosh across the screen. This gives your animation actions weight and heft, and leaves your audience clear as to what is going on in the piece.

Music

I cannot emphasise enough how important picking the right music for your animation is to the finished piece.

The music you select will have your audience either in tears or reaching for the volume button.

Depending on whether it's library music or composed especially for your animation, the soundtrack will typically come into the process at different points. Your studio team needs to think about the tone of the script and match the music accordingly, for example, something sober but pacy for a technical piece, or an evocative melody for a sensitive subject.

The absolute ideal is to have music written for your animation, as then the composer can perfectly match the mood to the content, writing in crescendos, volume and tone to fit with the narrative of the animation itself. This way, the music is dictated by the narrative and can be fashioned accordingly.

Due to common corporate budget constraints, animation studios tend to use a variety of royalty-free music libraries to pick a style that matches the animation in tone, substance and length. Approaching the music in this fashion, the team needs to pick a track before the animation is created, so that the action in the animation can work together with the musical track.

CASE STUDY – WINDSOR CINEMA

salamandra.uk was approached by Windsor's new cinema, The Screen, at The Old Court, Windsor's Community Artspace, to create an introductory animation short to start each movie showing. The cinema team wanted an animation that would captivate audiences and look sleek and modern, with a nod to the traditional and retro elements of film, the historic town and the iconic architecture of the converted fire station venue.

After a robust briefing and re-briefing process, my team and I distilled a concept for our client, embracing their vision and transforming an idea into digital life, with a look which encompasses the clean and modern *and* cinema history. The sound design that accompanies this animation is evocative and descriptive, and accounts for 50% of its success.

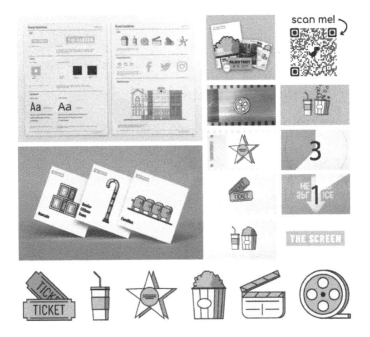

The retro sounds of the celluloid film getting reeled through the projector, the clapperboard, the slurping of a fizzy drink and subtle popcorn sounds, followed by a shushing voice gets the audience ready and settled.

Then the final number countdown sounds, and the musical ident at the end finishes the piece and announces
the start of the movie experience.

You can view it here: www.salamandra.uk/our-work/screen

Rendering

Rendering is used in both 2D and 3D computer-generated
animations. It's the process of getting the final assembled
animation scenes or pieces out of the computer in the
form of a sequence of individual pixel-based frames.

For 3D, rendering is the process of turning information
from a 3D model into a 2D image. It can be used to
create a variety of images, from intentionally nonrealistic
to photorealistic. Here, the term 'rendering' defines the
automatic process of generating digital images from
three-dimensional models by means of special software.

Depending on the size of the files and the length of your
animation, rendering can be a long process. Render times
are central processing unit (CPU) and project dependent.
Just as a fast CPU and large random-access memory help
your studio's computers run smoothly, video cards with
fast graphics processing units and plenty of onboard
memory will render graphics quickly and efficiently.

Because rendering is so hardware and software intensive,
and takes a long time to work through, it is quicker and
more effective for your animation studio to use render

farms (a high-performance computer cluster, built to render CGI for film and TV). Unless, of course, they're using a real-time render engine, which negates or significantly reduces render times.

A fifteen-second render of a particularly detailed and high-definition animation can take a few days, so consider timelines and deadlines upfront, as well as budget. Render farms can be costly for large files, particularly if there is a short deadline and the service needs to be condensed.

Editing

The editing process is where your studio pulls the main bones of the animation together so the content and flow are right for your narrative and convey your complex messages memorably. Editing can also be an undervalued role, but it takes great skill and flair to get it right cohesively, on brief, with pace and flow.

There is limited editing involved in animation, as your studio will animate and render things to the exact length they need to be, dictated by the storyboard, as compared to rolling film footage, where there will usually be lots of takes that will need to be cut together. The exception is, of course, if your studio team is doing a motion graphic edit with lots of different footage, in which case editing will be an important component.

Compositing

Compositing is the process or technique of combining visual elements from separate sources into single images or animation to create the illusion that all those elements are part of the same scene. Compositors create the final image of a frame, shot or visual-effects (VFX) sequence by taking all the different digital assets used, such as computer-generated images, live-action footage and background paintings, and combining them to appear as one cohesive image or shot. VFX is the process where imagery is created or manipulated outside the context of a live-action shot in film production, integrating live-action footage and computer graphics to create realistic imagery.

Because your studio may have several animators working on different parts of your animation, the visual elements all need to be threaded together into one whole scene or set of scenes, with transitions between each section. This is one reason why compositing is required. Additionally, animation tends to be worked up in layers or scenes split into different compositions to keep the (often hundreds of) layers organised and usable. Compositing also includes adding additional effects, layers or colour correction over the top of all of the sequences once they're compiled.

For 3D animations, every scene tends to be rendered in multiple layers or render passes, which will be reunited in the compositing stage. Compositing is the first step in

3D animation post-production, taking the render passes from the production stage, combining them together and mixing in additional adjustments, images or layers to create a more cohesive composition.

The compositing stage can save huge amounts of time and money in a 3D animation studio. The tools and techniques available to compositors make it possible to adjust the look of a project without having to re-render it, which would be a lengthy and costly process.

Exporting

Once your animators have combined all of the elements we've discussed in this chapter and produced a final cut that they are happy with, they will get to the exporting of your video.

There are a lot of particular settings and configurations that result in different file formats and qualities – depending on the end use of your video. Your studio team will be able to help you determine what you will need based on your request. For example, whether the animation is for use online, at an event or on TV will dictate the resolution, file type and frame rate it requires.

The resolution simply means how many pixels the video is made up of. You may be familiar with the terms '1080p' or 'Full HD', which simply mean the video is 1,920 pixels wide by 1,080 pixels high, the standard output for regular video uses online. Where your animation needs to be displayed on a larger resolution screen, you might need the video exporting at 4K or 3,840 pixels wide by 2,160 pixels high, especially when your studio will be rendering from 3D. Your animation team will need to know this at the start of the animation process.

The most common file type your studio will discuss with you will be mp4, the most common video format and the main one used online. Additionally, .mov files provide high-quality, but very large file sizes. Your studio can provide this, if needed for your project. If you are creating animated content for an event with huge screens of an irregular size and shape, there are some alternative formats such as HAPQ. Rest assured, these can be provided, too, usually at the request of your audio-visual technicians, for use in specialist projection software.

Summary

In this chapter, we have touched on the sound, music, rendering, editing, compositing and exporting processes of animation. These technical elements are vital to the creation your project. When done well, they will bring your finished animation to life to engage, delight and entertain your audiences. And when it comes to creating a memorable and immersive audience experience, remember that sound is just as important, if not more so, than the content of your animation.

chapter 9

Placement

Now you have your shiny new animation, the next step is to decide how to use it, where to house it and how and where to post or share it. Creating your asset is only half the job; you need to ensure that you repurpose, leverage and 'sweat' it.

Wearing both creative and business hats, a good animation studio team will craft you a memorable animation *and* advise you on all the ways you can use it to get the optimum bang for your buck. You can then take one simple asset and set it to work to give you the best possible marketing ROI.

Which channel will you use for your animation's dissemination? I will list a few for you in this chapter, including your website, social channels, presentations, email signatures and communication vehicles for sales and HR.

Distribution

Your corporate explainer animation can be placed on your company website landing page, so that your visitors 'get' in a snap what you offer. This is marketing gold because your messages are absorbed via an asset that is engaging and memorable to your target audiences, and using video on your website exponentially improves your SEO. Win-win!

Video helps your SEO due to the time the viewer is on the site and building back links, with the caveat that the video does not slow down the page speed. This can have a negative effect, particularly with users of mobile devices, and you will lose your audience.

I encourage you to have a full-screen explainer animation on your landing page versus one that needs people to click on it to start it. When it comes to your web audience engagement, the fewer clicks, the better, so work with your web developer to make the video a centre piece or focal point on your landing page that plays automatically. If the piece is too large to do this effectively, get it to play a snippet with a button to invite viewers to play the full animation, such as on www.salamandra.uk

According to a study by Cisco, 'Globally, business internet video traffic will be 70% of business internet traffic in 2021, up from 51% in 2016.'[47] Facebook users are 39% more likely to share, 36% more likely to comment on and 56% more likely to 'like' an online video versus a text-only article. Getting that interaction is a positive signal for search engines of the value of your content. This will increase the likelihood of your animation being found and drive traffic to your site – currently, Facebook averages more than 4 billion video streams per day.

With 65% of people being visual learners, according to molecular biologist John Medina, vision is our most dominant sense, taking up half of our brain's resources.[48] Apart from the obvious social media platforms where you can post your animation, there are several sales, marketing and communications uses it can have, too. These include it being used by your internal audiences, such as your HR department as part of their induction, educational programme or health and safety training to introduce new or prospective employees quickly and succinctly, and excite them about your business.

So much information can be included in your animation, it's perfect for lead generation, because prospects absorb a lot by viewing it. This means that they can ask your team pertinent in-depth questions that lead to a sale, rather than lots of general questions about the basics of your business, allowing for a shorter sales cycle, a quicker conversion and better marketing ROI.

As an asset, an animation will give your sales team more confidence, because it helps them to focus more on the prospect while ensuring that all the essential points relating to the business have been covered by the ani-mation. They can use the time the prospect is watching the animation to observe their body language to see if they are interested, and if so, which parts of the animation trigger the best response. Usually, the prospect's feedback is that the video was instructive, engaging, funny, emotional, or whatever approach you originally planned for it, and your internal teams will instantly see how effective this marketing and educational tool is for your business.

Your video can easily be cut up into sections of three- to five-second animations that can be re-used to highlight different topics, services or products. They can also showcase the different areas of the website, or accompany an article, electronic white paper or blog on a certain topic. Any good studio will work with you to extract as much as you can from one animation.

Short animations are great for populating your social media posts as engaging moving visuals to support topics, messages or announcements, informing and building up your followers. Post your animation to YouTube or Vimeo's open platforms for a bigger reach with links back to your website for SEO gains. You can use the YouTube link within your email signature and, depending on your email platform, it will appear as a thumbnail at the bottom of your missive, enticing your audience to press play and experience your corporate explainer. It's like including a mini-TV advert with every email you and your team send.

The animation can, of course, be used as part of a TV campaign. As long as your studio team knows all the platforms on which you intend to use it up front, they can create all the elements required in the finished piece to enable you to adhere to the channel's requirements.

CASE STUDY – PARITY TRUST TV ADVERT

Parity Trust, the only charity in the mortgage industry, asked salamandra.uk to create an animated TV advert to illustrate its flexible affordable loans and mortgages for the older age group or those who do not naturally fit into the traditional lending criteria.

We created a standout cardboard-style TV advert animation for Parity Trust to convey its services and complex messaging. This advert was then aired on TV on a tailored timeline, based on the time of day and geographical location chosen to reach the charity's target audience. The precision of the airing slots, reflecting the right demographic's watching habits, made the campaign highly targeted and more affordable, and because of this, Parity Trust enjoyed a healthy ROI.

Today, TV advertising is within the reach of small businesses. Take a look at our work with Parity Trust at www.salamandra.uk/our-work/paritytrust

Animated presentations

Never have there been so many eyes on screens! When the Covid-19 pandemic forced huge populations of the world to remain indoors, businesses profited from a seemingly captive audience. And they continue to profit;

my inbox is full of 'You're invited to a webinar' and 'Join us for a virtual chat' messages. Having accepted many of these invitations, I can't help but think that while they're interesting, there is more that can be done with the content by using an animated presentation.

By animated presentation, I don't mean basic PowerPoint animations such as the infamous fade transition; I mean presentations that make your brand look a million bucks. With slick motion graphics, animated elements and sound design, these PowerPoint presentations not only stand out from the crowd, they also make your brand memorable to your target audience.

I'm sure we've all been there: sitting in a stuffy room or on Zoom, trying to stay focused on a pitch, product explanation, sales forecast etc while suffering through a 'death by PowerPoint' scenario. Most people don't have the time to put into making their presentations visually effective, and often just show text and a couple of pie charts.

A study conducted at the University of New South Wales by John Sweller found that showing people the same words that are being spoken reduces, rather than increases, audience comprehension.[49] In other words, when you throw up bullet points, and then run through them, you're pretty much guaranteeing that no one will remember what you're covering. It's not necessarily because you're boring; it's because most people can't read and listen at the same time.

PowerPoint came out in 1990, so by now, we should be way past sending our audience to sleep with uninspiring slides and mediocre imagery that don't portray our business in the best light. If the aim of a presentation is to make your brand memorable or provide valuable information to either internal or external clients, then it has to leave a lasting impression on your audience.

Visuals in motion are key. Including motion graphics in your presentation will increase the amount your audience retains and leave a positive lasting impression of your brand, showing that your company is not the same as the rest out there. You can use the animations sparingly, peppering them throughout the presentation, or you can go the full hog and animate the whole deck, creating a clickable but flowing presentation that feels like you're watching a film.

You can also get your animation studio to design the presentation to be used on multiscreens with different animations going on in each for a more epic impact. This can be re-created in a virtual 3D auditorium for Zoom meetings or conferences.

CASE STUDY – MILWAUKEE ELECTRIC TOOL

Milwaukee Electric Tool uses animated presentations for its yearly Europe, Middle East and Africa (EMEA) conferences. This is a power tools manufacturer that has an unwavering commitment to the trades and continues to lead with a focus on providing innovative trade-specific solutions. As such, Milwaukee Electric Tool likes to use cutting-edge presentations for its events. The Milwaukee team wanted salamandra.uk to eclipse previous years with one of the most impressive animated multiscreen presentations we'd made so far. They were delighted with the powerful end result.

The power tool giant invites its 3,000+ suppliers to an annual conference in a different location and country every year, to share its sales, projected figures and new products. For its Monaco conference, Formula One and the Grand Prix were huge influencers of our final creation, with an outstanding forty-five-minute 'clickable' presentation across eighteen screens. Having so many screens showing different animations on the stage floor, surrounds and ceiling allowed for a more immersive experience, adding a 'reveal' type transition for products and secondary animation for the company's trademark lightning and explosions marketing treatments.

To create this impactful piece, we needed to take into account the venue's floor plan. Once we had all of our planning in place, we worked backwards from the final screen layout, ensuring the animation would flow smoothly from one screen to the next in real time to accompany the speeches, as well as be clickable on demand. With the impactful visuals and sound completely surrounding the audience and drawing their focus for a multidimensional experience, it was a presentation on steroids.

You can take a look at www.salamandra.uk/our-work/millwaukeeprodvis

Professionally animated PowerPoints are still in the sweet spot of being used by industry leaders, but not yet common in the business sphere. This means that the businesspeople who are using them stand out from the crowd.

With growing numbers of people making the transition into the digital business world, businesses need to use online presentations for events such as webinars, conferences, product launches, sales pitches and showcases, many of which are essential for keeping them afloat. From huge projection-mapped shows where the presentation is beamed onto different sized screens to 3D product previews, animated presentations run like a slick interactive video. As a marketeer, how do you make sure you are generating quality leads? Presentations, webinars, conference calls and virtual networking are the answer.

Research shows that 73% of B2B marketing and sales leaders say webinars are the best way to generate high-quality leads, because the average webinar attendee session is nearly an hour long.[50] No other content drives that kind of engagement, so make your webinars look smart by adding motion to your images. Bear in mind your age demographic – 73% of those involved in B2B research and decision making are millennials, who are digital natives and spend an average of 7.2 hours online each day, with 2.4 of these spent watching videos. And over a third of these people are the sole decision maker. To market effectively, you must know and understand your buyer profile from various generations and their preferences for absorbing information.

Summary

Now you have your shiny new animation, the next step is to decide how and where to use it. Which channel will you use for its dissemination? A good animation studio team will advise you on all the ways you can get the optimum bang for your buck. As long as your studio team knows all the platforms on which you intend to use it up front, they can create all the elements required in the finished piece in the required format.

With more and more people working remotely and connecting online, there's a 'captive' audience out there that companies are looking to engage. Brands will need to shape their normal activities and turn them into remote ones, including meetings, briefings, expos, demos, conferences, webinars and all the other business activities that used to require face-to-face time.

We all now have the opportunity of putting spellbinding animated content out there that can transport your audiences to new environments and worlds to see and experience technology first-hand, as well as enabling their experience to be personalised and tailored to their requirements. This will bypass a lot of the old-fashioned sales cycles, allowing you and your customers to jump straight into the sexy bits of the process where they will experience the brand, product or service in a way that has never been possible before.

○ chapter 10

The Future Of Animation

In his fascinating book *Why We Sleep*,[51] Matthew Walker notes that at least one-third of our brain is built for vision and visual usage (clearly a necessity in our ongoing survival); how fitting this is for the business environment, where we can visually inform and memorably train our target audiences using static or animated images.

In the medium of animation, there are constant innovations taking place. All the software is continuously evolving and improving, becoming more flexible and diverse in its usage with new add-ons or devices to be explored. The number of platforms that animation can be created for and used on is also growing, from the original entertainment to corporate explainers and education in the Internet of Things, the military, space travel and aeronautical training stations, virtual conferencing, children's education, pharmaceuticals and massively growing and profitable gaming programs. According to the *Digital Market Outlook*, the revenue in the global Download Games segment is forecast to be 24.120,8 million US dollars by 2025.[52] And if these industries are embracing animation to get their complex messages across, then B2B enterprises of any size can do so too.

Most of our social and business communications have now moved online, so smart brands are choosing new ways to bridge the gap between meeting clients face to face and on the plethora of digital platforms. They are already finding an alternative to running events by using VR cost effectively in their offering. With the increasing popularity of working from home and online socialising, this is a golden opportunity to use animation to upgrade all forms of internal and external communications.

Let's have a closer look at the new technology landscape for animation.

AR

AR means we're seeing the real world through a device with virtual 3D elements or animation projected on to the environment around us. Because of this platform's adaptability to so many environments and uses, it is currently at the forefront of business, experiential and educational discovery and innovation.

Previously, this technology could only be used via a smartphone or tablet, but it has expanded into wearable devices such as smart glasses, sometimes called wearable computer glasses. This gives a more hands-on user experience (UX) outside of the confines of the small screen, enabling it to be integrated in our everyday lives. It's particularly popular in games.

Smart glasses superimpose information on top of what the wearer sees through an optical head-mounted display or a transparent heads-up display, found on some newer car windscreens. The user can manipulate 3D projections of objects with eye tracking, voice commands or hand gestures. This opens the doors to digital design for creating anything from a work of art to a piece of engineering, along with enabling those with disabilities, because with smart glasses, the user can work hands free and incorporate smartphone apps such as GPS tracking and navigation.

AR can be used for remote training or on-the-job troubleshooting. Even risk-averse sectors such as pharma are now taking on this new approach.

CASE STUDY – PHARMA

salamandra.uk worked with a major UK pharmaceutical on a campaign using AR to explain to clinicians about the development, symptoms and treatment of an infant illness. The animation of a child's progressive illness is an emotive experience that resonates immediately with the clinicians and brings the message home succinctly and memorably. Our client, a parent himself, on viewing the first iteration of the animation became quite moved by what he was seeing and sensed immediately that it would work in his market.

Our 3D animation, hosted on a pharma platform and viewed via AR through a tablet or phone, allows the viewer to 'anchor' it within their actual environment and resize it while it unfolds. This enables them to walk around the piece and view its 360-degree development.

The animation shows an infant in his cot becoming sick and showing symptoms of the illness's time-lapsed progression. The child is then seen in a hospital cot with all the medical paraphernalia around him as his illness gets progressively worse. The campaign served to highlight a less well-known illness and its indicators to clinicians.

The campaign started in the UK, and because of its success, it was localised for EMEA, Australasia and then globally. We made different cultural variations of the child depending on region, which contributed to how much viewers related to the scene and the ultimate success of the campaign. Because of the development stages of the medical content, this animation is still under a nondisclosure agreement.

Now used in many B2B as well as B2C industries, AR is a surprisingly approachable animation platform. Previously considered expensive, it has come a long way in terms of development and affordability and has many exciting new uses. It allows brands to give customers a unique experience by tapping into their mobile devices, offering them a 'try before you buy' option with augmented shopping experiences for anything from sunglasses to lipstick colours.

AR can improve B2B sales by offering a more in-depth experience of the product, even allowing customers a 360-degree view and interactivity with the brand, right down to zooming into the product's microscopic detail. You can use QR codes digitally or in print to launch your animated message automatically, or you can use any background image, logo or business card to unleash the animation.

For more ideas, check out www.salamandra.uk/our-work/augmented-reality

VR, mixed reality (MR) and extended reality (XR)

VR, an equally exciting platform, requires (at the time of writing) a headset to view the animation. This allows the viewer a virtual 360-degree created experience which can be passive or interactive. A passive experience can still have the viewer sitting on a paraglider, for example, and seeing all the way around them as they fly up and down. Ahead, behind, beneath, above – it's all encompassing. And with hand controllers, users can engage with their surroundings for an interactive demo experience, for example to practise elements of using machinery or equipment to practise for their job, or to play out different HR or sales scenarios.

Unlike AR, which allows the user to see their real world through a device with superimposed virtual animation on top of it, VR immerses them in a totally created virtual world. It can be used for virtual conference stands with product demonstrations or to preview designs scaled to real life-sized environments and depth before products even enter the production phase. This is called digitisation, and it saves businesses huge amounts of time and investment in creating new products. To make this totally virtual experience feel more real and believable to our brains, it's essential for the animation to look believable and built 3D environment to use textures, lighting and fine details.

VR is perfect for an immersive learning environment. If your employees work in confined or hard-to-reach spaces, such as deep-sea oil rigs, and you need to train them up on how to work in these environments, VR animation will give the user as real an experience as possible without putting them in danger or blowing the travel budget. This technology is a fantastic tool for health and safety, firefighting and any other types of training for dangerous tasks or occupations and is why it is used so much in the forces and in aeronautics.

VR still has teething problems. Some users experience vertigo or travel sickness when using it because of the optical illusion of moving or being at extreme heights, for example. Designers are working to understand why this discomfort happens and how to ameliorate the experience for all.

These technologies allow you to create experiences where users can interact with your products virtually or visit distant exhibitions, conferences, concerts, museums, funfair rides and even escape room games without having to travel long distances physically, saving money *and* the environment. Win-win! They also create an opportunity for your company to provide a more immersive brand experience for your customers. It's a new frontier for branded content and business animated narratives.

CASE STUDY – ETON COLLEGE

The salamandra.uk team and I were invited to exhibit at our local rather famous school, Eton College's annual careers fair, but instead of having a traditional stand, we opted for a virtual one using VR. Consequently, we had a long line of students, 'beaks' (Eton slang for teachers) and other exhibitors wanting to put on the headsets and try out the virtual world on offer.

The space included giant 3D salamandra.uk lizards, our logo, as part of the furniture, with our branding and animation reel playing within a giant picture frame over a blazing fireplace in the palace-like interior. Via the controls, viewers could have a go at shooting targets using bows and arrows and guns, while being entertained in a kinaesthetic sight and sound experience.

VR can be used by charities to create more empathy from donors, placing them in the environment that the charity is trying to improve or bring awareness to, such as taking them inside refugee camps. This creates a feeling of human experiential interaction and increases the donor's willingness to support the initiatives. A good example is the experience using film and animation to immerse the viewer in a VR piece about Grenfell Tower. Take a look at www.channel4.com/collection/grenfell-our-home

MR, sometimes called hybrid reality, is the merging of real and virtual worlds. The Microsoft HoloLens blends 3D holographic content with the physical world, allowing animated holograms a real-world context and scale so users can interact with them while still viewing the real world. Excitingly, XR combines all three technologies, AR, VR and MR, amalgamating them to offer your customer a computer-generated experience that may even include physical reality. Imagination is limitless. It's what makes us human.

The new normal

The Covid-19 pandemic brought many changes to the way we work and the landscape has been forever transformed into a 'new normal'. People have permanently changed their ways, from working to attending meetings, conferences or expos remotely. This behaviour necessitates connecting mostly online.

In this world of increased screen time, your brand will need to stand out from all the two-dimensional content to keep engaging your audiences and avoid screen fatigue. Animation in all its dimensions will open up continuous opportunities for you to create fresh experiences, visually delighting your audience and conveying your complex messaging, because the only limit is your and your studio's imagination.

Advertising will be easier and more cost effective, with remote animation specialists replacing costly and virus-risky in situ film crews, where all health and safety measures need to be in place. Content creators worldwide have seen a huge uptake in the use of animation for adverts, entertainment and education, both on TV and on most online platforms. Voiceovers can be spoken in any language, making these assets territory mobile and easy to localise.

Conference presentations

How can your business run conferences remotely online while still offering pizzazz in a modern and innovative fashion? AR can bring the virtual element you are portraying into your audiences' own space, whether during the presentation using QR codes on screen or on any printed or digital collateral used to advertise the event, or afterwards in blogs and articles. You can create virtual auditoriums with multiscreens for your presentations and host live virtual Zoom-style calls in a 3D environment. These are effective in creating the feeling for your clients that they are at an international conference facility, when in fact they are sitting in their home office, at their dining room table or in the kitchen.

Interactive real-time animations

Animation technology developers, in both software and hardware, are in a race to bring innovation to platforms. Some examples are Unreal Engine and Unity platforms, originally created to build computer games. These can offer the user unprecedented interactivity in real time, such as changing the language used by all the characters, the season of the story or the outcome of the narrative while watching the narrative unfold. Similar to the Netflix series *Black Mirror: Bandersnatch*, where viewers could pick different outcomes to the narrative throughout the episode.

There is so much exciting potential for interactive animations now, such as creating emotive narrative experiences for brands to help viewers feel more connected to the story. The biggest benefit for this would be in training, where viewers can watch an animation and see the direct consequences of their choices, and then replay the animation making different choices and experiencing different outcomes. This really reinforces the learning, whether you are training your clients on how to use your product or service in the pre-sales, sales or post-sales part of your cycle, or coaching your staff on how to work safely and efficiently.

Additionally, interactive explainer videos could offer viewers a more personalised experience, allowing them to discover the information that is most applicable to their needs and tailoring the flow of the narrative based on the options or services they pick as the animation plays out.

This will add to the effectiveness of animation as a sales tool by involving viewers more directly, so they will intrinsically feel more emotionally connected to the outcome they play a part in creating. This emotional connection is a vital way to create a memorable and trust-building experience for customers.

Interactive real-time animation provides the opportunity to globalise content instantly – increasingly important in this online age. If your animation is playing using real-time technology, the user could change the language of on-screen graphics or audio, the ethnicity of the characters, or even the geographical setting with the click of a button as the animation continues to play. Rather than having a collection of videos in each language if your animation needs to be published across a number of territories, you could have one interactive animation with all of the options built in seamlessly.

Animation can be used to show a product visualisation with exploded view, or show the product assembling together, or demonstrate configurations or uses. With an interactive animation, viewers can pan around the product, viewing it from any angle as it animates, or dictate the flow of the demonstration, moving through the narrative when they are ready.

The future applications of interactive animation in business are endless and extremely valuable. There will be considerable uptake of this option as it becomes ever more attainable for marketing.

Summary

There are now more exciting technologies for animation applications at our business fingertips than ever. And with remote working becoming increasingly popular, technology will allow us to continue to take strides in delighting, engaging and informing our target audiences. It will also become essential to our internal communications, from HR inductions and ongoing staff training, to business meetings, sales pitches, VIP stand invitations, virtual expo stands and global webinars.

The future's virtual. The future's animated.

Conclusion

Animation is important. It enables us to create narratives and communicate emotions and ideas in a way that is unique and easy to perceive and digest for any age or target market.

In *Destination Animation*, I have taken you through why animation is a phenomenal and indispensable B2B marketing tool, and how to navigate your way to creating your own corporate animation. We've explored how to follow the three Ps of plan, produce and publish to ensure a successful animated project that provides you with your all-important marketing ROI.

Animation helps to connect audiences throughout the globe in hybrid ways that are here to stay. B2B animation can capture your customers' imagination and transport them to different virtual worlds, even during face-to-face engagement or live-action or hybrid events. They can enter a new realm of sensory and emotional or hyper-realistic animations that educate, inform and explain a plethora of complex messages in a way that stays in their long-term memories. Animation is just like a visual jingle.

Now is a perfect time to benefit from animation. I encourage you to include it in your marketing mix, whether it is to explain what you do or remotely engage with your internal team, clients, suppliers, the media and all your target audiences. An animation can be created remotely from anywhere in the world. It can be seamlessly updated and adapted for a growing number of uses and platforms.

Use the 3Ps process to build your own successful multiuse end asset that can be placed on a myriad of platforms. Distil your message verbally, visually and auditorily, picking out what resonates with your target audience and conveying how your product or service will mitigate their pain points.

Innovations in AR, VR, MR and XR have important implications for business, users and marketeers, offering new ways to sell and train across geographies and using avatars to engage when face to face is not possible or economical. It's onwards and upwards in how animation is continuing to help your business take your branding to the next level and convey your complex messages visually and memorably. Nothing communicates as succinctly as an animation, and now you are armed with all the information you need to embark on commissioning one successfully to create the best possible asset for your business.

If you would like to investigate the exciting world of animation more, I recommend your read *The Illusion of Life: Disney animation* by Ollie Johnston and Frank Thomas,[53] and *The Animator's Survival Kit* by Richard Williams[54] to complement all you have learned in *Destination Animation*.

An exciting future awaits. Let's get animated!

Notes

1   J McQuivey, 'How video will take over the world' (Forrester, 2008), www.forrester.com/report/How+Video+Will+Take+Over+The+World/RES44199

2   C Harrington, 'What we can learn from Dropbox's famous explainer video' (Idea Rocket, 2015), https://idearocketanimation.com/6164-can-learn-dropboxs-famous-explainer-video

3   Simpleshow, 'Imagery vs text: which does the brain prefer?' (World of Learning, 2015), www.learnevents.com/blog/2015/09/07/imagery-vs-text-which-does-the-brain-prefer

4   Z Johnson, '20 Fun Facts About Snow White and the Seven Dwarfs on Its 80th Anniversary' (e-online, 2017), www.eonline.com/news/901665/20-fun-facts-about-snow-white-and-the-seven-dwarfs-on-its-80th-anniversary

5   L Hamilton *Brave New Girl: How to be fearless* (Orion Spring, 2016)

6   L Fullerton, 'Millennials make 73 per cent of purchasing decisions in B2B, survey notes' (The Drum, 2016), www.thedrum.com/news/2016/06/08/millennials-make-73-cent-purchasing-decisions-b2b-survey-notes

7   R Robinson, 'The Realities of VR and AR in the Industry' (PharmaVoice, 2019), www.pharmavoice.com/article/2019-06-ar-vr

8   C Petrov, '45 virtual reality statistics that will rock the market in 2021' (Techjury, 2021) https://techjury.net/blog/virtual-reality-statistics

9   Simpleshow, 'Imagery vs text: which does the brain prefer?' (World of Learning, 2015), www.learnevents.com/blog/2015/09/07/imagery-vs-text-which-does-the-brain-prefer

10 'Video marketing statistics: The state of video marketing in 2021' (Biteable.com, 2021), https://biteable.com/blog/video-marketing-statistics/

11 www.cisco.com/c/en/us/solutions/executive-perspectives/annual-internet-report/index.html

12 'Cisco Visual Networking Index: Forecast and Trends, 2017–2022' (Cisco, 2017), https://twiki.cern.ch/twiki/pub/HEPIX/TechwatchNetwork/HtwNetworkDocuments/white-paper-c11-741490.pdf

13 'Top Video Marketing Statistic 2021' (Explain Ninja, 2021), https://explain.ninja/blog/20-video-marketing-statistics-2020

14 'Mask' (The Animation Workshop, 2015), www.youtube.com/watch?v= R1vnFfTaLAA

15 'Stop, Think, Dignity', Skills for Care 2D animation (YouTube, 2014), www.youtube.com/watch?v=VSunLDv4zyM

16 'Video Marketing Statistics 2020' (Wyzowl, 2020), www.wyzowl.com/ video-marketing-statistics

17 'Video Marketing Statistics 2020' (Wyzowl, 2020), www.wyzowl.com/ video-marketing-statistics

18 K Deepasha, '9 Facts That Show Videos Are Getting More Prominent in the SERPs' (Unamo, 2017), https://unamo.com/blog/seo/9-facts-that-show-videos-are-getting-more-prominent-in-the-serps

19 K Shelton, 'The Value Of Search Results Rankings' (Forbes, 2017), www.forbes.com/sites/forbesagencycouncil/2017/10/30/the-value-of-search-results-rankings/?sh=6c59782744d3

20 K Shelton, 'The Value Of Search Results Rankings' (Forbes, 2017), www.forbes.com/sites/forbesagencycouncil/2017/10/30/the-value-of-search-results-rankings/?sh=6c59782744d3

21 M Bowman, 'Video Marketing: The Future Of Content Marketing' (Forbes, 2017), www.forbes.com/sites/forbesagencycouncil/ 2017/02/03/video-marketing-the-future-of-content-marketing/? sh=4721af046b53

22 '[Infographic] Video Advertising in Numbers' (Incubata nmpi, 2016), https://nmpidigital.com/infographic-video-advertising-in-numbers

23 '[Infographic] Video Advertising in Numbers' (Incubata nmpi, 2016), https://nmpidigital.com/infographic-video-advertising-in-numbers

24 'How To Keep Online Viewers Watching Your Video' (First Focus, 2016), www.firstfocus.nyc/video-marketing/keep-online-viewers-watching-video

25 ImageThink, 'Is it True or False that vision rules the brain?' (ImageThink, 2012), www.imagethink.net/true-or-false-vision-rules-the-brain

26 C Liu and P Elms, 'Animating student engagement: The impact of cartoon instructional videos on learning experience' (Association for Learning Technology, 2019) https://journal.alt.ac.uk/ index.php/rlt/article/view/2124

27 'Studies Confirm the Power of Visuals to Engage Your Audience in eLearning' (Shift Learning, 2014), www.shiftelearning.com/blog/ bid/350326/studies-confirm-the-power-of-visuals-in-elearning

28 www.artofthetitle.com/title/alien

29   www.artofthetitle.com/title/stranger-things

30   www.artofthetitle.com/title/catch-me-if-you-can

31   www.artofthetitle.com/title/mozart-in-the-jungle-season-4

32   www.artofthetitle.com/title/the-incredibles-2

33   www.artofthetitle.com/title/lemony-snickets-a-series-of-unfortunate-events/

34   www.artofthetitle.com/title/marco-polo/

35   www.artofthetitle.com/title/game-of-thrones/

36   www.artofthetitle.com/title/black-sails/

37   www.artofthetitle.com/title/the-crown/

38   www.artofthetitle.com/title/black-panther/

39   www.artofthetitle.com/title/the-walking-dead-season-9/

40   www.artofthetitle.com/title/anne/

41   J Clement, 'Global video game market from 2020 to 2025' (Statista, 2021), www.statista.com/statistics/292056/video-game-market-value-worldwide

42   'BlackRock Client Customizations Interactive Videos' (Magnet Media) https://magnetmediafilms.com/work/project-blackrock-client-customizations-interactive-videos

43   'How to Increase Your App Downloads With Video Trailers' (DumbLittleMan.com, 2018), www.dumblittleman.com/how-to-increase-your-app-downloads

44   R DellaFave, 'Marketing Your Indie Game: The Single Most Important Thing to Learn' (gamedevelopment.tutsplus.com, 2014), https://gamedevelopment.tutsplus.com/articles/marketing-your-indie-game-the-single-most-important-thing-to-learn--gamedev-7157

45   '10 killer app store marketing tips' (Slideshare, 2016), www.slideshare.net/maorgad/10-killer-app-store-marketing-tips

46   The foley process is named after Jack Donovan Foley who, before the advent of sound libraries, created many sound effect techniques used in filmmaking. He is credited with developing a unique method for performing sound effects live and in synchrony with the picture during a film's post-production stage. Professionals in this trade are called Foley artists.

47   'Global – 2021 forecast highlights' (VNI Complete Forecast Highlights), www.cisco.com/c/dam/m/en_us/solutions/service-provider/vni-forecast-highlights/pdf/Global_2021_Forecast_Highlights.pdf

48   'Why Animated Video is the Best Strategy for Your Social Media'
      (Dreamgrow, 2018), https://www.dreamgrow.com/animated-video

49   G James, 'Harvard Just Discovered That PowerPoint Is Worse Than
      Useless' (Inc.com, 2019), www.inc.com/geoffrey-james/harvard-just-
      discovered-that-powerpoint-is-worse-than-useless.html

50   A Tiffany, '10 Webinar Benchmarks Every Marketer Should Know'
      (Goto.com, 2019), www.goto.com/blog/7-webinar-benchmarks-every-
      marketer-should-know

51   M Walker, *Why We Sleep: The new science of sleep and dreams*
      (Penguin, 2018)

52   Statistica, 'Forecast of Video Games revenue by segment in the
      World from 2017 to 2025' (Digital Marketing Outlook, 2021),
      www.statista.com/outlook/digital-markets

53   O Johnston and F Thomas, *The Illusion of Life: Disney animation*
      (Hyperion, 1997)

54   RE Williams, *The Animator's Survival Kit* (Faber & Faber, 2009)

Acknowledgements

It seemed a good idea to write a book, particularly on something I love, to help B2B marketeers and entrepreneurs understand and plot their own animation journey. But actually putting it together and writing it was quite a different 'story'. I couldn't have done it without the enormous help from my team at salamandra.uk, my beta readers, my adventurous clients and my lovely publishers. In my thanks, I will endeavour not to forget anyone.

This book wouldn't have happened without the stupendous detailed help, suggestions, editing and rewriting, and illustrating from salamandra.uk's polymath art director, Emma Rhodes. When I flagged, she took up the baton, closely followed by our marketing guru Abbie Scrimgeour. Her faultless and meticulous feedback on the content ensured it had enough of a marketing and branding focus.

Thank you to the illustrious Kate O'Connor, Executive Chair at Animation UK Council, who so graciously agreed to be a beta reader and then write a fantastic foreword for the book, lending it our industry's gravitas and clout! I could not be prouder of this – thank you!

I would like to thank my super bright and talented long-term friend and consultant Vanessa Vasani for her incisive feedback and unimpeachable logic to help me improve the business content and narrative. John McMahon of MCM was a huge help in giving super-fast, useful, honest and supportive feedback, for which I'm very grateful. If a book is judged by its cover, then I owe my thanks to Fred Watts for creating the wonderful 3D illustration of our mascot Sal getting ready to board an underground train for his own *Destination Animation* and to Nicholas Francisco for his nod to Disney with my adapted author's photo, taken by talented Eton photographer Graham Keutenius! I also need to thank our creatives Jessie Delatousche and Janine Getty for helping with the illustrations.

Keeping me sane during the writing process were the members, not already mentioned, of the salamandra.uk studios, known as the lizard lounge, including Marcus Bowler, Samantha Dunn, Georgia Barr, Jordan Lloyd, Luis Massarela, Sylvia Bourhill, Alisa Schroeder, Zander MacKay and Miles Trompetto.

I'd like to thank all salamandra.uk's lovely clients who have made our company's journey possible. There are too many to mention, but I appreciate you all. My company would not be where it is today without the support, inspiration, networking, opportunities and advice offered by Daniel de la Cruz previously from Agency Collective, Spencer Gallagher, Peter Hoole, Abbe Wheeler and Mark Probert from Agencynomics, Stephen Knight from Pimento, Oliver Lingwood-Craddock and team from the Supper Club, Clive Mishon from Alliance of Independent

Agencies, Kate O'Connor from Animation UK and Neil Hatton from UK Screen Alliance.

I need to thank my publishers, Rethink Press, particularly Lucy McCarraher and Joe Gregory for making this journey a possible and manageable process. And many thanks to Alison Jack for doing the unenviable task of meticulously editing this book, and Kerry Boettcher for seeing it through the production process.

I'd like to thank my family for putting up with me during the writing of this book: my husband Lochmar, whose patience and support have been unfailing, and my grown-up children Zander and Cara, who have always been my company's biggest fans and supporters. Thank you.

Throughout my life, I've been lucky to be inspired and supported by the creativity and drive of my concert pianist mother Lillian MacKay and her opera singer sister Jennifer Smith – both talented, driven and stimulating women. Also by the fortitude, humour, entrepreneurialism and dedication to family and country that my father Captain John MacKay inspired in all of us. I'd like to thank my brother Stuart MacKay for his sense of adventure and fun, and my sister Sandra MacKay for her whip-smart humour, kindness and inimitable story and joke telling.

And last, but not least, I'd like to thank you, the reader, for making it this far in the book. I hope you enjoyed it and that your passion for animation will grow to match ours at the salamandra.uk lizard lounge.

The Author

Christine MacKay founded salamandra.uk in 2014 to specialise in animation for B2B and visual problem solving. Having worked both client and agency side on three continents, she has become an expert in building collaborative teams and strong company culture, business development and cross pollinating businesses as a serial networker. Her team works as visual problem solvers across eighteen different industries, from children's books to corporate explainers. salamandra.uk now has animation studio presence in Eton, Dundee and San Francisco.

Christine has always had an affinity for imagery, from her first childhood crush on cartoon character *Marine Boy*, to a deep emotional response eliciting welling eyes at Botticelli's Primavera in Florence. This love for imagery has been with her throughout her career and decades of travelling, and after falling in love with animation while working in New Zealand, she decided to run with her passion and founded salamandra.uk.

Christine is an international award-winning creative visual problem solver, entrepreneur, Royal Television Society and Alliance of Independent Agencies animation awards judge and chair, Cannes Lions See it Be it mentor, and international speaker and author. She is a member of Animation UK, Animation Women UK, Eton Community Association, London Scotland House, Pink Shoe Club, Agencynomics, Little Black Book Online, Dundee and Angus Chamber of Commerce, a lifetime honorary member of The Agency Collective, a supporter of Resource Productions, and was named as one of Britain's top 100 female entrepreneurs by f:Entrepreneur #Ialso. Her business was listed in the Small Biz 100 for 2020, and her studios have been recognised by a multiple of national and international awards.

Christine founded The Tech and SaaS Multimedia Marketing Meetup group and co-founded The Pharma Multichannel Marketing Meetup group. Both regular events, they are vehicles to grow communities and get brands, marketeers and agencies together to share learnings and case studies on current trending topics.

Find out more and connect with Christine:

🌐 www.salamandra.uk

🔗 www.linkedin.com/in/salamandradesigndigital

🐦 @salamandrauk

📘 salamandrauk